PRESCHOOL
CRAFT▸PLAY

Group
Loveland, Colorado

Preschool Craft-Play

Credits
Contributing Authors: Jody Brolsma, Robin Christy, Kathy Duggan, Nanette Goings, Lois Keffer, Susan L. Lingo, Lori Haynes Niles, and Mary Van Aalsburg
Book Acquisitions Editors: Mike Nappa and Susan L. Lingo
Editor: Liz Shockey
Creative Products Director: Joani Schultz
Copy Editor: Debbie Gowensmith
Art Director/Designer: Lisa Chandler
Cover Art Director: Liz Howe
Cover Designer: Helen Lannis
Computer Graphic Artist: Joyce Douglas
Illustrator: Sharon Holm
Production Manager: Ann Marie Gordon

Unless otherwise noted, Scriptures quoted from The Youth Bible, New Century Version, copyright © 1991 by Word Publishing, Dallas, Texas 75039. Used by permission.

Library of Congress Cataloging-in-Publication Data
      p.   cm.
    ISBN 1-55945-610-8 (alk. paper)
    1. Education, Preschool—Activity programs. 2. Handicraft—Study
and teaching (Preschool)   I. Group Publishing.
LB1140.35.C74P74   1996
372.5049—dc20   95-45599
                                                                                 CIP

10 9 8 7 6 5   05 04 03 02 01 00 99
Printed in the United States of America.

Contents

Spring Specials

Summer Spectaculars

Holiday Happenings

Introduction

Kids love crafts. And kids love games and activities. Wouldn't it be great if unique craft ideas were combined with lively games, songs, rhymes, and other activities? That's just what Group has pulled together for you in this fun new book! *Preschool Craft-Play* offers more than 100 creative crafts that are just like preschoolers—they don't sit still! These unique craft projects are easy and fun for preschoolers to make and are designed to be played with again and again.

Most craft idea books contain run-of-the-mill ideas for projects that end up on the refrigerator or forgotten in a drawer. Not the craft ideas you'll find in *Preschool Craft-Play!* In the pages of this book, you'll find exciting ideas such as cookies in a bag, shimmering fabric leaves, pop-up puppets, fly-swatter paintings, and much more. But that's just the beginning! Each craft idea is accompanied by a special game, song, action rhyme, or other snappy activity your preschoolers will love. Crafts and playtime—what could be more fun for lively preschoolers?

Preschool Craft-Play offers crafts and activities that are
- process-oriented, not product-oriented;
- teacher-friendly and require little, if any, teacher preparation;
- age-appropriate and require no scissors for children to handle; and
- geared for preschool fun and frolic.

So get ready to offer your preschoolers fresh fun with creative crafts they can play with again and again!

HELPFUL HINTS

Here are some clever cleanup ideas and other helpful hints to make any craft project easier:

- Make paint shirts in a snap by cutting holes for arms and heads in paper grocery sacks.
- A dab of rubbing alcohol removes permanent marker from laminated plastic table tops.
- Keep extra craft items such as paper plates, sponges, tempera paint, brushes, cotton swabs, glue, and lunch sacks in a colorful craft box for handy, spur-of-the-moment projects.
- Remove dried glue and paint from table tops by placing wet paper towels on the dried material for a few minutes then using a plastic ice scraper to scrape the material away.

PART 1

Fall
Festivals

Autumn Harvest Place Mats

CRAFTY TIPS

✔ Tape place mats to drinking straws and wave them as flags in a jaunty Apple Parade. Supply lively marching music and invite children to parade around the room.

✔ Try stamping apple prints on sturdy cotton or burlap fabric to create delightfully textured "doilies" which will last for years.

SIMPLE SUPPLIES

You'll need newspaper; white construction paper; paint pans; a knife; apples; clear, self-adhesive paper; scissors; glue; paint shirts; and red, yellow, and green tempera paint.

DIRECTIONS

❶ Before class cut three apples in half and save the seeds. You'll also need to cut out an 8½ ×11-inch piece of clear, self-adhesive paper for each child. Leave the backing on the self-adhesive paper.

❷ Cover a table with newspaper. Set out paint pans each containing ¼ inch of tempera paint. Place an apple half in each pan and set out white construction paper.

❸ Have children wear paint shirts or paper grocery sacks with holes cut out for arms and heads. Show children how to dip the apple halves in paint then blot them on newspaper to remove any excess paint. Have children stamp the apple halves on their white papers in pretty designs.

❹ When apple prints are dry, let children glue a few apple seeds on the corners of the papers. Then carefully seal each "place mat" with clear, self-adhesive paper. Be sure children's names are written on the backs of their place mats.

Do this just-for-fun action rhyme with children while their place mats are drying.

EXTRA FUN

If I were an apple seed *(squat down small)*,
I'd grow up to be *(stand up slowly)*
A big, round apple *(circle arms over head)*
In a strong, tall tree. *(Stand straight and tall.)*
Then someone would pick me *(pretend to pick an apple)*,
Me-oh-my! *(Hold hands to cheeks in surprise.)*
And I'd make a dee-li-cious *(rub tummy)*
Apple pie! *(Pretend to hold a pie.)*

Everlasting Leaves

SIMPLE SUPPLIES

You'll need fresh leaves, aluminum foil, scissors, self-adhesive magnetic tape, a plastic bowl, white craft glue, water, a spoon, hinge-style clothespins, paintbrushes, a blow-dryer, and newspaper.

DIRECTIONS

❶ Before class mix equal portions of white craft glue and water in a small plastic bowl. Cut a 1-inch strip of self-adhesive magnetic tape for each child. You'll also need to tear off a 10-inch square of aluminum foil for each child.

❷ Cover a table with newspaper. Set out the glue mixture, hinge-style clothespins, and leaves. Hand each child a square of aluminum foil.

❸ Show kids how to clip clothespins to the leaves, then dip the leaves into the glue mixture. Help children use paintbrushes to remove excess glue then lay the leaves on the squares of foil.

❹ Let kids take turns blowing warm air on the leaves with a hand-held blow-dryer to speed up drying time. Be sure the dryer speed is set on low.

❺ When the leaves are dry, remove the aluminum foil and clothespins, then add strips of magnetic tape to the back of the leaves to make magnets!

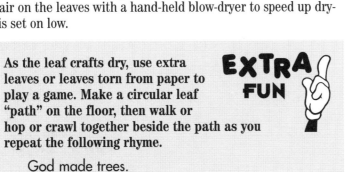

As the leaf crafts dry, use extra leaves or leaves torn from paper to play a game. Make a circular leaf "path" on the floor, then walk or hop or crawl together beside the path as you repeat the following rhyme.

> God made trees.
> God made leaves.
> God says, "Please
> Take care of these!"

EXTRA FUN

CRAFTY TIPS

✔ Everlasting leaves spark great discussions about God's changing world and help illustrate the concept of everlasting life.

✔ Stir glitter into the glue mixture for a different effect.

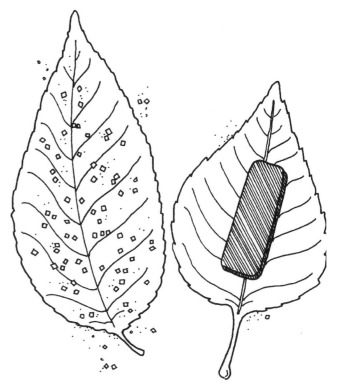

9

Edible Pumpkin Patches

CRAFTY
TIPS

✔ This candy dough works well with plastic candy molds. Let children mold candies in holiday shapes then give the candies as gifts.

✔ Refrigerated candy dough will stay fresh for up to one week.

SIMPLE SUPPLIES

You'll need ⅔ cup of sweetened condensed milk, 4½ cups of powdered sugar, orange and green food coloring, two resealable bags, and paper towels.

DIRECTIONS

❶ Before class mix and knead the powdered sugar and condensed milk until they make a soft, pliable dough. Knead orange food coloring into two-thirds of the dough and green food coloring into the remaining portion of dough. Store the dough in separate resealable bags.

❷ Have children wash their hands, then give each child a paper towel and walnut-sized lumps of orange and green dough.

❸ Encourage children to make 10 small orange pumpkins with green stems—or to use their imaginations to create green pumpkins with orange stems! Before children gobble their pumpkin patches, sing the song in the Extra Fun activity.

EXTRA FUN

Have the children point to their candy pumpkins as they sing this song to the tune of "Ten Little Indians."

One little, two little, three little pumpkins,
Four little, five little, six little pumpkins,
Seven little, eight little, nine little pumpkins,
Ten roly-poly pumpkins!

Sing the song again and let children count the "pumpkins" on their fingers. On the last line, have children roll across the floor on their sides.

Bible-Times Tops

SIMPLE SUPPLIES

You'll need newspaper, a bag of large marshmallows, chocolate-kiss candies, pretzel sticks, canned frosting, plastic knives, and paper plates.

DIRECTIONS

❶ Before class cover a table top with newspaper. Place canned frosting, pretzel sticks, marshmallows, and plastic knives on the table.

❷ After children wash their hands, hand them each a paper plate, a large marshmallow, a pretzel stick, and a chocolate-kiss candy.

❸ Show children how to poke a pretzel stick about halfway into a marshmallow.

❹ Help children spread a small amount of frosting on one end of their marshmallows.

❺ Let children unwrap the chocolate candies and push the flat end of the candies onto the frosting to complete their edible spinning tops.

❻ Invite children to make two edible tops: one to eat now and one for the Extra Fun activity. Let the candy tops dry for 10 minutes before playing the game.

✔ Edible tops are great for learning about what it was like when Jesus was a little boy.

✔ Use the tops as part of a lesson about children around the world.

Explain to the children that the candy tops are like wooden toys the Hebrew children played with long ago. Point out that Jesus may have played with a wooden top.

EXTRA FUN

Let children practice spinning their tops on the paper plates. Have older children in your class spin the tops in pairs. When a top stops spinning, have the person the pretzel stick points to tell his or her name.

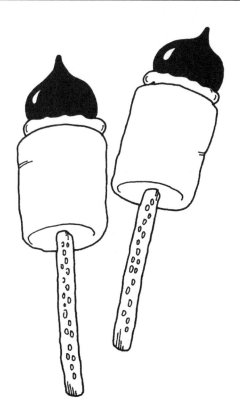

My Fine Friends

CRAFTY TIPS

✔ Let the children make life-size paper dolls of themselves.

These dolls work well with lessons on growing up or how God created each of us to be special and unique.

✔ You may want to display the fine friends and invite parents to "meet" them.

SIMPLE SUPPLIES

You'll need white shelf paper; markers; crayons; scissors; cotton swabs; pie pans; glue; and small scraps of yarn, ribbon, felt, and wrapping paper.

DIRECTIONS

❶ Before class cut white shelf paper into 4-foot sections. You will need one section for each child.

❷ Place the shelf paper on the floor. Have the children lie down on their papers while adult helpers trace around each child.

❸ Set out crayons, markers, pans of glue, and other decorating items.

❹ Encourage children to use cotton swabs dipped in glue to add yarn, ribbon, felt, and wrapping paper for hair, clothes, and other decorations. Use crayons and markers to make smiling faces.

❺ Have adult helpers cut out each fine friend for the Extra Fun activity.

EXTRA FUN

Let the children move about with their Fine Friends as they sing this song about friendship. Sing the song to the tune of **"Row, Row, Row Your Boat."**

Love, love, love your friends;
Share your toys and play.
Say kind words and do nice things—
Be happy all the day.

"The land has given its crops. God, our God, blesses us" (Psalm 67:6).

Pretzel Weavings

SIMPLE SUPPLIES

You'll need large, twisted pretzels; 1-inch-wide craft ribbon; and scissors.

DIRECTIONS

❶ Before class cut one 3-foot length of ribbon and two 1-foot lengths of ribbon for each child.

❷ Gather children around a table. Let each child take a 3-foot length of ribbon and five pretzels (plus a few extra pretzels to munch).

❸ Demonstrate how to weave the ribbon from behind the edge of one pretzel, over the center twist, then behind the opposite edge of that pretzel. Repeat this process for the next four pretzels so they're woven side by side.

❹ When each child has woven the ribbon through five pretzels, have him or her carefully slip the pretzels to the center of the ribbon with an equal length of leftover ribbon at both sides.

❺ Have adult helpers and children work together to add 1-foot ribbons at each end then tie bows at each end to make wall hangings.

EXTRA FUN

Let children have fun getting all twisted up like pretzels with this active game.

Help children find partners who are similar in height. Have partners face each other and clasp their hands overhead. Show them how to keep their hands clasped and turn a complete circle by facing away from each other then facing each other again. You may want to have races to see which pairs can twist and turn all the way from one end of the room to the other end.

CRAFTY TIPS

✔ Point out that when pretzels were first made, their unusual shape was meant to look like children whose arms were crossed in prayer. Explain that we often give special prayers of thanks in the fall for all the good crops farmers are harvesting.

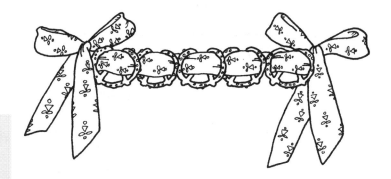

Apple Swags

CRAFTY TIPS

✔ Dried apple slices may become brittle, so caution children to handle them carefully. Cracks can be mended almost invisibly with transparent tape.

✔ You may want to outline the "heart" in the center of the dried apples with red glitter glue.

✔ Serve an apple-sample snack. Set out slices from four or five different varieties of apples and let children choose which they like best.

SIMPLE SUPPLIES

You'll need dried apple slices (see instructions below), pencils, a 3-foot length of jute twine or narrow ribbon for each child, and liquid apple-spice potpourri.

DIRECTIONS

❶ About two days before class, cut vertical slices from the centers of Red Delicious apples. (The skin of Red Delicious apples remains bright red even when dried, and the deep top and bottom crowns create a lovely heart shape when the apples are sliced in the center from the stem down.) You should get three to five center slices from each apple.
Brush the apple slices with lemon juice on both sides, place them on cookie sheets, and let them dry in a 200-degree oven for about 24 hours. Turn the apples over two or three times during the drying process. When they are dry, punch two holes in each slice using a sharpened pencil or knife.

❷ Gather children around a table. Give each child at least three apple slices and a length of jute twine or ribbon.

❸ Show children how to weave the twine in and out of the holes, using an unsharpened pencil to poke the twine through.

❹ Tie the ribbon at each end of the swag into bows.

❺ Let children put a drop of liquid potpourri in the center of each apple slice.

EXTRA FUN

Remind children that apples and all the other good things we eat come from God. Then teach children this fun, rowdy thank you rhyme.

> Apples go "crunch" *(one big clap on "crunch")*
> When I munch, munch, munch. *(Use hands to make munching "mouths.")*
> I love apples! *(Make a big "apple" with arms overhead and jump three times.)*
> Thanks a whole bunch! *(Clap three times.)*

Glittering, Golden Leaves

SIMPLE SUPPLIES

You'll need newspaper; glitter glue; gold paint pens; cotton swabs; tape; paint shirts; a blow-dryer; and orange, yellow, and brown construction paper.

DIRECTIONS

❶ Cover a table with newspaper. Set out the construction paper, glitter glue, gold paint pens, and cotton swabs. (Gold paint pens may be found in craft stores.)

❷ Invite children to tear two or three large leaf shapes from the construction paper.

❸ Have children put on paint shirts or paper grocery sacks with holes cut out for arms and heads. Let children decorate their leaves with gold paint pens and small amounts of glitter glue.

❹ Tape the leaves to a table and have children take turns blowing the leaves with a blow-dryer to speed drying time. (Be sure dryer speed is set on low.) Mention that wind blows real leaves to the ground in autumn.

When the leaves are dry, let children sing this action song to the tune of "Twinkle, Twinkle, Little Star." Invite children to use their leaves as they sing.

Glitter, glitter, little leaves *(flutter the paper leaves),*
Swaying, swaying in the trees. *(Wave the leaves above your head.)*
Colors, colors all around *(wave the leaves above your head),*
Tumble, tumble to the ground. *(Let leaves float to the floor.)*
Glitter, glitter, little leaves *(flutter the paper leaves),*
Blowing, blowing in the breeze. *(Wave the leaves above your head.)*

CRAFTY TIPS

✔ Make a tree trunk and limbs from twisted brown paper, then tape it, using masking tape, to the wall. Let children choose one of their glittery leaves to tape to the tree.

✔ Use this craft during a lesson on changing and growing. Leaves change from green to gold but still remain leaves.

✔ Make sure paint-pen marks are completely dry before handling the leaves.

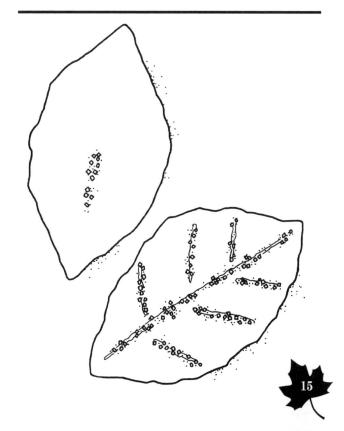

15

Scarecrow Socks

CRAFTY TIPS ✔ Set out a variety of items children can choose from to decorate their scarecrows, such as fabric scraps, glitter glue, and colored paper.

✔ To make scarecrows "scarier" to birds, you may give children yarn to attach jingle bells or old keys to the bottom of the scarecrows.

SIMPLE SUPPLIES

You will need old nylon hosiery, scissors, permanent markers, puffy paint, black construction paper, 10-inch lengths of yarn, fiberfill, a darning needle, and glue.

DIRECTIONS

❶ Before children arrive cut the legs off nylon hosiery (unless you're using knee-high hosiery), saving the lower-leg sections.

❷ Set out all other items on a table.

❸ Give each child a section of hosiery and a ball of fiberfill about the size of an apple. Show children how to stuff the fiberfill into the hosiery. Help them push it tightly to the end of the hosiery and tie a length of yarn under it.

❹ Invite children to make faces for their scarecrows by tearing off small pieces of the black construction paper and gluing them in place. They may glue on lengths of yarn for hair, make a puffy-paint smile, or draw a face with markers.

❺ As children finish have them bring their scarecrows to you. Use a darning needle to string a length of yarn through the top of each scarecrow's head, then tie off the yarn. Explain that children can hang their scarecrows from a tree near a garden or flower bed.

Have children hold their scarecrows while you lead them in the following rhyme.

EXTRA FUN

Five fat crows were sitting in a tree,
Thinkin' 'bout stealing my corn from me!
My little scarecrow jumped with a roar.
One crow flew away;
Then there were four.

Four fat crows were sitting in a tree,
Thinkin' 'bout stealing my corn from me!
My little scarecrow jumped with a whee!
One crow flew away;
Then there were three.

Three fat crows were sitting in a tree,
Thinkin' 'bout stealing my corn from me!
My little scarecrow jumped with a "boo!"
One crow flew away;
Then there were two.

Two fat crows were sitting in a tree,
Thinkin' 'bout stealing my corn from me!
My little scarecrow jumped and said "Run!"
One crow flew away;
Then there was one.

One fat crow was sitting in a tree,
Thinkin' 'bout stealing my corn from me!
My little scarecrow jumped and said "Yum!"
That crow flew away;
Now there are none!

Bumpy Apple Sachets

SIMPLE SUPPLIES

You'll need fine-grain sandpaper, scissors, white paper, crayons, cinnamon oil or vanilla, an iron, and an old towel.

DIRECTIONS

1 Before class cut the sandpaper into apple shapes. Be sure each sandpaper apple is at least 3 inches across. You'll need one sandpaper apple for each child.

2 Set out crayons. Give each child a sandpaper apple and let children scribble-color the apples with crayons. Encourage children to press hard while coloring. As children color their apples, heat the iron to low. Be sure the iron is out of the children's reach.

3 When the apples are colored, hand each child a sheet of white paper, then help children fold the papers in half. Demonstrate how to slide a sandpaper apple between the fold.

4 Place the folded papers containing the colored apples under a towel. Iron gently over the towel for 30 seconds. Make sure preschoolers do not touch the iron!

5 Let children unfold their papers to reveal "bumpy" apple pictures. Then invite children to put a drop or two of scented oil on their sandpaper apples to make them smell good.

EXTRA FUN

Play this game after the sandpaper apples are ironed and scented. Sing the words to the tune of "London Bridge." Form the branches of an apple tree by holding your arms out in front of you. Encourage children to hold their Apple Sachets as they walk under the branches while you sing. Gently catch two of the children in your "branches," then let them form another tree to walk under. Continue until each child has been a "tree."

Apples now are falling down,
Falling down, falling down.
Apples now are falling down *(drop the apples)*;
Pick them up! *(Pick up the paper apples.)*

CRAFTY TIPS

✔ Use Bumpy Apple Sachets with lessons about harvest, fruits of the spirit, or even the story of Adam and Eve.

✔ These scented sandpaper apples make great sachets for dresser drawers or the family car.

✔ Enjoy a snack of apple slices dipped in flavored yogurt or chocolate sauce to spice up your "apple adventures."

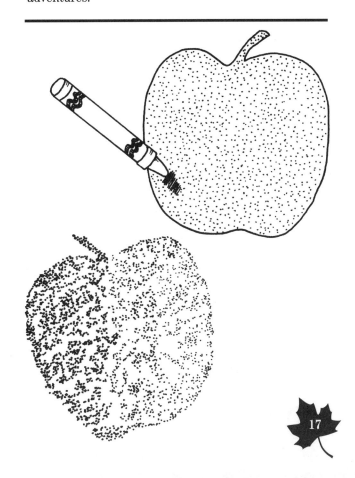

17

Ollie Owls

CRAFTY TIPS

✔ With a few changes, the owl pattern may be adapted to use as Christmas angels or shepherds.

✔ Use this craft idea with lessons about wisdom and understanding. Let the owl represent listening and patience.

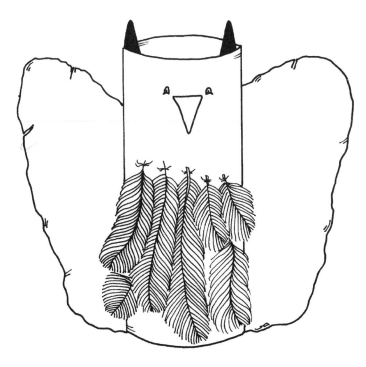

SIMPLE SUPPLIES

You'll need empty bathroom-tissue tubes, scrap construction paper in orange and brown, brown paper grocery sacks, craft feathers, markers, glue sticks, scissors, and tape.

DIRECTIONS

❶ Before class cut small, ½-inch triangles from orange and brown construction paper. Each child will need one orange triangle and two brown triangles. If you don't have empty bathroom-tissue tubes, make 6-inch tubes from poster board.

❷ Set out markers and glue sticks. Give each child a cardboard tube. Have children draw eyes on the top half of the tube. Mention to the children that they're going to make hoot owls.

❸ Distribute the orange and brown construction paper triangles. Tell children to glue an orange triangle below the eyes for the beak then glue the brown triangles as ears.

❹ Set out craft feathers. Show children how to glue craft feathers to the bottom half of a tube as chest feathers for an owl.

❺ Let children tear wings from the paper grocery sacks then tape the wings to the owl. Now Ollie Owl is ready to sit, fly, and say wise things!

EXTRA FUN

Say this rhyme while the children hold their owls like finger puppets and "fly" them around the room.

Who? Who? Who loves you?
Jesus, he's the one.
Who? Who cares for you?
Jesus, he's God's Son. Yeah.

Fabric Leaf Prints

SIMPLE SUPPLIES

You'll need a variety of real leaves, lunch sacks, aluminum pie tins, newspaper, acrylic fabric paints, 12-inch squares of muslin, paint shirts, and paper towels. You'll also need unopened cans of vegetables or fruit.

CRAFTY TIPS

✔ Leaf prints make wonderful decorations for T-shirts, windsocks, and many other fabric projects.

DIRECTIONS

❶ Be sure to have a 12-inch square of muslin for each child. Men's cotton handkerchiefs work great with this craft idea.

❷ Take children on a leaf-gathering expedition. Hand out small lunch sacks and encourage children to find five or six different varieties of leaves. If you don't have access to real leaves, you may purchase and use silk or plastic leaves.

❸ Cover tables with newspaper. Have children put on paint shirts or paper grocery sacks with holes cut out for arms and heads.

❹ Place fabric squares around the table. Set out pie tins containing fabric paints. Have each child stand by a square of fabric.

❺ Help children experiment with different ways to place the leaves on their fabric.

❻ Demonstrate how to paint a leaf and press the painted side onto the fabric. Show children how to roll a heavy can over it to make a clear print.

❼ Help children remove each leaf after pressing it. Let them place the used leaves in the center of the table for others to share. Preschoolers can do this process themselves, but it's wise to have extra adult helpers on hand to help children dispose of their leaves and clean their fingers before they use another color of paint. The prints should be dry enough to take home within an hour.

EXTRA FUN

Ask the children who made the trees and leaves. Then teach them this action rhyme to celebrate God's wonderful leaves. Let them hold their dry leaf prints as they twirl around in place.

Leaves, leaves, leaves *(turn around in place)*
Up the street and down. *(Point one way then the other.)*
Leaves, leaves, leaves *(turn around in place)*
Flying all around. *(Twirl arms overhead.)*
Leaves, leaves, leaves *(turn around in place)*
Flutter to the ground. *(Gently toss leaf prints in the air.)*

"And also use the shield of faith with which you can stop all the burning arrows of the Evil One" (Ephesians 6:16).

Shiny Shields

CRAFTY TIPS

✔ Use this craft to help children learn about God's protection and care.

✔ Let children hold their shields as they sing "I'm in the Lord's Army" or when they're learning about the armor of God.

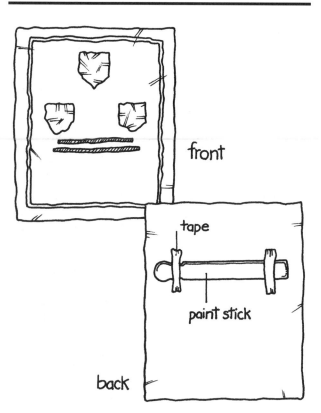

front

tape

paint stick

back

SIMPLE SUPPLIES

You will need paper grocery sacks, scissors, paint-stirring sticks, transparent tape, crayons, and aluminum foil.

DIRECTIONS

❶ Before class collect a wooden paint-stirring stick for each child. (Paint-stirring sticks are available free at most paint and hardware stores.) You'll also need to cut the bottoms from paper grocery sacks, then cut the sacks vertically in half. Cut one paper-sack "shield" for each child.

❷ Set out crayons, transparent tape, and small pieces of aluminum foil. Hand each child a paper shield. Invite children to use crayons to decorate their shields then tape bits of shiny foil to the shields to make them really shine!

❸ Help each child securely tape a paint stick across the back of his or her shield. Place tape only at the ends of the paint-stirring sticks so children can slide their hands around the center of the sticks to hold their shields.

Play this action game to let kids try out their Shiny Shields. EXTRA FUN

Hand each child a half-sheet of newspaper to crumple. When you say "go," have kids toss the paper wads at each other and hold up the shields to deflect the flying paper. Toss the paper "arrows" again and again for a few minutes, then ask children to toss their arrows in the wastebasket.

"You must celebrate the Feast of [Harvest]. Offer to God the first things you harvest from the crops you planted in your fields" (Exodus 23:16).

Scarecrow Smocks

SIMPLE SUPPLIES

You'll need large paper grocery sacks, pinking shears, glue, tape, fabric scraps, and straw or raffia.

DIRECTIONS

❶ Before class use pinking shears to trim colorful fabric scraps into 1-inch triangles and rectangles. Turn grocery sacks upside down. Cut up the middle of the front, cut a neck hole from the top, and cut armholes in the sides to make smocks.

❷ Set out the paper smocks, glue, tape, and fabric shapes. Place straw or raffia on the table. Let each child choose a smock and several fabric scraps.

❸ Help children glue the fabric scraps here and there on their smocks then tape bits of straw or raffia around the necks and armholes.

❹ Make sure all the children have their initials somewhere on their smocks. Help children put on their Scarecrow Smocks.

Talk about scarecrows and how they guard gardens and crops so greedy blackbirds don't gobble up the growing food. Have children wear their Scarecrow Smocks and prance around after they have learned this scarecrow rhyme.

Prance, scarecrows, prance! *(Prance around the room.)*
The crows don't have a chance. *(Shake your head.)*
When we wave "hi" *(wave your hands)*,
Away they fly! *(Flap your arms.)*
Prance, scarecrows, prance! *(Prance around the room.)*

CRAFTY TIPS

✔ Use face paint and a variety of old hats to enhance your scarecrow costumes.

✔ Take photos of all your little scarecrows and make copies for parents.

Shepherd Walking Sticks

CRAFTY TIPS

✔ Use this craft idea in a lesson about Jesus as our shepherd. Talk with children about how the shepherd takes care of the sheep, and relate that to how God takes care of us.

✔ Make Shepherd Walking Sticks during your Christmas lessons.

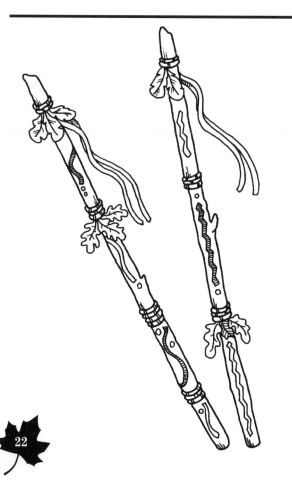

SIMPLE SUPPLIES

You'll need sticks or 2-foot dowels, colored vinyl tape (or masking tape if colored tape is not available), colorful yarn, markers, leaves, and craft feathers.

DIRECTIONS

❶ Before class collect a 2-foot-long stick for each child. (You may purchase and use 2-foot dowels if sticks aren't available.) Cut several 8-inch lengths of colorful yarn for each child.

❷ Set out colored vinyl tape or masking tape, yarn, markers, leaves, and craft feathers.

❸ Hand each child a stick. Mention that they'll make walking sticks like the ones shepherds use in their fields to help them walk up and down hills as they care for their sheep.

❹ Show the children how to tape leaves and feathers to the sticks. Help children wrap and tie yarn to their walking sticks.

❺ Give children markers to further decorate and personalize their walking sticks.

EXTRA FUN

Mention that shepherds used walking sticks to help keep their sheep in the fields. Sing this shepherd song to the tune of "Ten Little Indians" while children march around with their Shepherd Walking Sticks. Have children tap their sticks on the floor each time you say a number.

One little, two little, three little sheep,
Four little, five little, six little sheep,
Seven little, eight little, nine little sheep,
Ten sheep in the field.

Pudding Pets

SIMPLE SUPPLIES

You'll need wax paper; vanilla instant pudding mix; a sealed plastic container; tape; a large serving spoon; paper plates; plastic spoons; and the following food items: raisins, marshmallows, cheese, grapes, cherries, and pretzel sticks.

DIRECTIONS

❶ Before class prepare the instant pudding mix following the instructions on the box. Place the pudding in the sealed plastic container.

❷ Cover a table with wax paper. Tape the wax paper's edges under the table to keep the paper in place. Set out paper plates containing the food items.

❸ Hand each child a paper plate and a plastic spoon. Use the serving spoon to put two spoonfuls of pudding on each plate.

❹ Tell children to use their plastic spoons to smooth the pudding on their plates in the shape of an animal's face.

❺ Show children how to use food items to make eyes, noses, mouths, and ears to create pudding pets on their plates. Encourage kids to tell what their pets eat, how they move about, what noises they make, and how big or little they are. Let kids enjoy eating their special treats after doing the Extra Fun activity.

CRAFTY TIPS

✔ Let kids make these animal faces then gobble the delightful treats during lessons on Noah's ark or Adam naming the animals.

✔ Substitute paper plates and pudding with rice cakes and peanut butter for a totally edible art project.

 **EXTRA FUN**

Before children gobble up their pudding pets, lead them in this action rhyme.

Of all the creatures
Great and small *(reach way up, then make yourself really small),*
I know my God
Has made us all. *(Outstretch hands to everyone.)*

Curly hair *(point to your hair)*
Or short or tall *(squat low, then stand tall),*
God will love us *(point up to heaven and God),*
One and all. *(Outstretch hands to everyone.)*

Bug Buddies

CRAFTY TIPS

✔ You may want to attach pieces of magnetic tape to the bottom of the bugs to create refrigerator magnets.

✔ Use this craft idea when talking about new life in the spring.

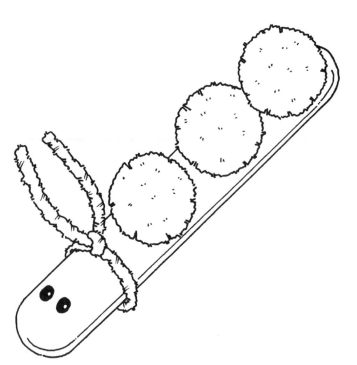

SIMPLE SUPPLIES

You'll need craft sticks, ¼-inch pompons, scissors, tacky craft glue, construction paper scraps, a hole punch, and chenille wires.

DIRECTIONS

❶ Before class use a hole punch to make pairs of "eyes" from construction paper scraps. Cut chenille wire into 3-inch lengths. You'll need one piece of chenille wire for each child.

❷ Set out the glue, pompons, and construction paper eyes.

❸ Give each child a craft stick and invite kids to create silly bugs. Help each child glue three pompons in a row on the craft sticks then glue a pair of paper eyes on one end of each "bug."

❹ Help children twist small chenille-wire antennae to their bugs.

❺ Encourage children to name their bugs and tell interesting things about them, such as what their bugs eat and where they live. Remind children that God made all living creatures—even the smallest bugs.

EXTRA FUN

While the glue is drying, lead children in playing Inchworm. Have children form a line, holding onto each other's waists. Tell children that they are inchworms. Stand in the middle of the room and call out instructions such as "Inchworm, walk to the window" or "Inchworm, hop up and down" or "Inchworm, tiptoe to the chalkboard." After each instruction has been carried out, have the leader go to the end of the line and allow the next child in line to be the leader.

"Thank the Lord because he is good. His love continues forever…He satisfies the thirsty and fills up the hungry" (Psalm 107:1,9).

Upside-Down Pumpkin Pies

SIMPLE SUPPLIES

You'll need newspaper, 8-ounce paper cups, plastic spoons, vanilla instant pudding mix, canned pumpkin, milk, cinnamon, cookie crumbs, and four bowls.

DIRECTIONS

➊ Cover a table with newspaper. Set out bowls of vanilla instant pudding mix, canned pumpkin, cookie crumbs, and cinnamon.

➋ Have children wash their hands. Give each child a paper cup and a plastic spoon.

➌ Help children mix three heaping spoonfuls of vanilla instant pudding mix, a sprinkle of cinnamon, and one spoonful of canned pumpkin in their paper cups.

➍ Pour milk in the paper cups until they're nearly full. Let children carefully stir the ingredients in their cups using the plastic spoons. Have children stir the mixture until it begins to thicken.

➎ Sprinkle cookie crumbs over the mixture. Invite kids to eat their Upside-Down Pumpkin Pies right away, or chill them in the refrigerator until the end of class.

CRAFTY TIPS

✔ Use Upside-Down Pumpkin Pies with lessons about harvest, Thanksgiving, the Feast of Weeks, or the Day of First Fruits.

✔ Let children omit the cinnamon or canned pumpkin if they desire. The Upside-Down Pumpkin Pies will still taste yummy without these ingredients.

EXTRA FUN

Do this fun action rhyme while your Upside-Down Pumpkin Pies are thickening.

Roll, little pumpkins, on the ground *(make rolling motions with your hands)*,
Forward, backward *(roll hands forward then backward)*,
Upside down! *(Peek between your knees.)*
Roll, little pumpkins, out at play *(make rolling motions with your hands)*,
Roll, roll, roll away! *(Lie down on your side, then roll across the floor.)*

Rock Families

SIMPLE SUPPLIES

You'll need paper lunch sacks, rocks, tacky craft glue, sturdy paper or plastic plates, newspaper, a hot-glue gun, a hole punch, and construction paper.

DIRECTIONS

❶ Before class use a hole punch to make lots of little "eyes" from colorful construction paper.

❷ Half the fun of this craft is in the gathering! Take children outside, give them each a lunch sack, and let them choose rocks to represent the people in their families. Have them place the rocks in their lunch sacks. Encourage children to choose larger rocks for parents and teenagers and smaller rocks for younger children.

Be sure the rocks are larger than a 50-cent piece to avoid any choking danger. If you can't collect rocks as a class, gather rocks before class and let children choose from a "rock pile."

❸ Cover a table with newspaper and hand each child a sturdy paper or plastic plate.

❹ Have each child position his or her rocks on a plate. Then have adult helpers hot-glue the rocks in place. Be sure children do not touch the glue gun or the hot glue. Allow the glue to cool for two minutes.

❺ After the hot glue has dried, let the children use craft glue to add construction paper eyes to each rock. Encourage children to tell about the people in their families as they work.

EXTRA FUN

Mention that families often come together at Thanksgiving and that families are something we can be thankful for. Have children stand in a circle holding their rock families. Teach them this family rhyme, then have children take turns introducing their rock families.

Big families, small families,
Families having fun.
Here is my own family,
Sitting all as one!

Harvest Bread

SIMPLE SUPPLIES

You'll need crackers; peanut butter; honey; paper plates; plastic bowls; spoons; plastic knives; and an assortment of grains and seeds such as sunflower seeds, rolled oats, bran, puffed rice, popped popcorn, and puffed wheat.

DIRECTIONS

❶ Before class pour grains and seeds in small bowls.

❷ Set out bowls containing seeds and grains. Place a spoon in each bowl. Give each child a paper plate with a few crackers and a plastic knife on it.

❸ Invite children to spread peanut butter or honey on their crackers. Then let children decorate their crackers by sprinkling them with grains and seeds.

❹ Talk about the different grains that are harvested and the foods children eat from these grains, such as corn bread, cereals, oatmeal, and muffins. Let children enjoy nibbling their healthful creations.

Bring in wheat, brown rice, millet, wheat berries, corn kernels, barley, soybeans, and different breads for the children to feel, smell, and taste.

Sing this song about the harvest to the tune of "The Farmer in the Dell."

It's harvest time in fall. *(Pretend to pick grain.)*
It's harvest time in fall. *(Pretend to pick grain.)*
Everybody, gather wheat. *(Put arms around each other.)*
It's harvest time in fall. *(Pretend to pick grain.)*

Let's grind the grains so fine. *(Pretend to grind grain.)*
Let's grind the grains so fine. *(Pretend to grind grain.)*
Mix and knead and bake the bread. *(Pretend to mix dough.)*
Let's grind the grains so fine. *(Pretend to grind grain.)*

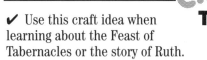

✔ Use this craft idea when learning about the Feast of Tabernacles or the story of Ruth.

✔ Glue leftover grain and seeds to paper plates for harvest collages.

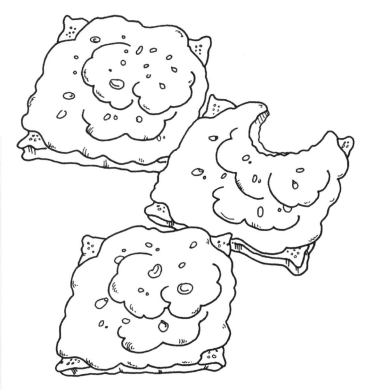

Fall Feely Boxes

CRAFTY TIPS

✔ Make "feely fabric boxes" from sensory scraps such as cotton balls, feathers, felt, fake fur, and burlap.

SIMPLE SUPPLIES

You'll need tacky craft glue; bits of ribbon, lace, and rickrack; and a small box for each child. You'll also need various nature items such as leaves, pine cones, twigs, flowers, grass, pebbles, and sand. You may want children to help collect these items.

DIRECTIONS

❶ Give each child an empty box. Then take children on a nature walk and invite them to collect items to fill their autumn boxes. Suggest items such as leaves, twigs, flowers, sand, pine cones, grass, and pebbles.

❷ Set out glue and bits of ribbon, lace, and rickrack. Have kids glue ribbon, lace, rickrack, and a few of their nature items to the outside of their boxes.

❸ Invite children to place the extra nature items inside their boxes. Talk about how the different items look and feel.

Let children hold their creations as they sing this nature song to the tune of "Did You Ever See a Lassie?" EXTRA FUN

Did you ever see a flower, a flower, a flower? *(Hold up hand with fingers extended like petals.)*
Did you ever see a flower blow this way and that? *(Sway from side to side.)*
God made all the world *(swing arms in big circle)*
For each boy and girl. *(Point to each other.)*
Did you ever see a flower blow this way and that? *(Sway from side to side.)*
Verse 2: Did you ever see a red leaf . . . fall this way and that?
Verse 3: Did you ever see a robin . . . fly this way and that?

"When we have the opportunity to help anyone, we should do it. But we should give special attention to those who are in the family of believers" (Galatians 6:10).

Pilgrim Hat Place Markers

SIMPLE SUPPLIES

You'll need plastic-foam cups, black crayons or markers, black construction paper, 3×5 index cards, craft glue, cotton swabs, pie pans, and gold glitter glue.

DIRECTIONS

❶ Before class cut a ½-inch slit in the bottom of each cup. Cut black construction paper into circles that are 2 inches larger than the top of the cups. Cut several 3×5 cards in half.

❷ Give each child a paper circle, a cup, and a black crayon or marker.

❸ Have children scribble black color all over their cups, leaving the rims of the cups white.

❹ Set out glitter glue and craft glue in pie pans. Show children how to dip cotton swabs in the glitter glue then make rectangles on the rims of the cups.

❺ Help children glue black circles to the openings on the paper cups to create brims on the "hats."

❻ While children are working, ask whose name they would each like on their place cards. Perhaps they'd like the name of a special guest who's visiting for Thanksgiving, or they might want the name of someone in their family. Write the name each child chooses on half of a 3×5 card. Show children how to slip the name cards into the slits in the top of the hats.

❼ Let children tell you what they know about Thanksgiving. Explain that the Pilgrims were people who loved God too.

> **Have children sit in a circle with their Pilgrim hats on their heads. Teach children this little thank you rhyme, then ask for a volunteer to tell something he or she is especially thankful for. Then have that child set his or her hat on the floor. Repeat the rhyme, then have another child tell one thing he or she is thankful for. Continue until each child has told a "thank you."**
>
> Thank you, God, for each one here,
> For friends and family far and near,
> And for bringing us Thanksgiving cheer.

EXTRA FUN

CRAFTY TIPS

✔ If you wish, you may spray-paint the cups with black paint before class.

✔ Encourage children to tell you other ways they can show kindness to friends and families during the Thanksgiving season.

29

PART 2

Winter Wonders

Bells of December

SIMPLE SUPPLIES

You'll need string; scissors; and red, gold, or white ¼-inch-wide ribbon. You'll also need two medium-sized jingle bells and a plastic berry basket for each child.

DIRECTIONS

❶ Before class thread string through the jingle bells and tie two bells inside the bottom of each berry basket. When the baskets are turned upside down, they'll look like chimes or bells. You'll also need to cut 6-inch lengths of ribbon. Cut at least five pieces of ribbon for each child.

❷ Set out the pieces of ribbon. Hand each child a basket bell. Help children weave the ribbon pieces in and out of the holes in the baskets.

❸ When children have finished weaving, help them make handles by tying large ribbon loops to the top of the bells.

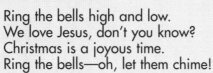

Celebrate the season with the Bells of December and the following action rhyme. Invite children to joyously ring their bells as you repeat the words to the rhyme.

> Ring the bells high and low.
> We love Jesus, don't you know?
> Christmas is a joyous time.
> Ring the bells—oh, let them chime!

CRAFTY TIPS

✔ Use the Bells of December craft idea to "ring in" the New Year.

✔ "Surround" the city of Jericho and use the Bells of December, instead of horns, to "ring" the walls down!

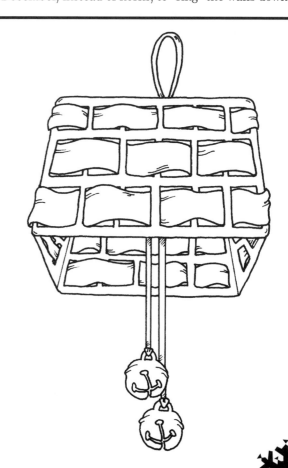

"They opened their gifts and gave him treasures of gold, frankincense, and myrrh" (Matthew 2:11b).

Spicy Sachets

CRAFTY TIPS

✔ Spicy sachets make perfect gifts, especially for Christmas, Valentine's Day, and Grandparents Day.

✔ Add an extra-special touch for Mother's Day. Make spicy sachets and glue ribbon, lace, buttons, and silk or dried flowers to the envelopes.

SIMPLE SUPPLIES

You'll need small envelopes, cotton balls, stickers, crayons, and vanilla or cinnamon oil.

DIRECTIONS

❶ Set out envelopes, stickers, and crayons. Invite children to decorate their envelopes with stickers and colorful crayon scribbles.

❷ Give each child three cotton balls. Have children hold the cotton balls while you put a couple of drops of vanilla or cinnamon oil on them.

❸ Have children slide the cotton balls inside the envelopes then lick the adhesive flaps and seal the envelopes.

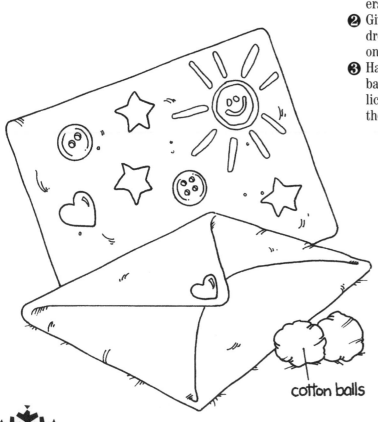

cotton balls

EXTRA FUN

Play this "nosy" game and sniff out some fragrant fun.

Gather items with an easily recognizable scent, such as a freshly cut orange, peppermint candy, bar soap, perfume, leather, cinnamon, and pine branches. Place each item in a brown paper bag. Choose one child to be the Sniffy-Sniffer.

Place a blindfold on the Sniffy-Sniffer and hold one of the bags under his or her nose. Ask the Sniffy-Sniffer to guess what's in the bag. Be sure each child has a turn being the Sniffy-Sniffer. Then have children sniff their spicy sachets and tell what things they like to smell, such as chocolate cake, fresh cookies, or Mommy's perfume.

"Who is this coming out of the desert like a cloud of smoke? Who is this that smells like myrrh, incense, and other spices?" (Song of Solomon 3:6).

Sweet and Scratchy

SIMPLE SUPPLIES

You'll need cinnamon sticks, Christmas cookie-cutters, crayons, ribbon, scissors, a hole punch, and medium-weight sandpaper.

DIRECTIONS

❶ Before class trace cookie-cutter shapes on the sandpaper. Cut out two or more shapes for each child.

❷ Set out cinnamon sticks, crayons, and a 12-inch piece of ribbon for each sandpaper shape.

❸ Give each child a sandpaper cutout and a cinnamon stick. Let children color the smooth side of their sandpaper cutouts.

❹ Show children how to rub the sandy side of their cutouts with the cinnamon sticks.

❺ Help children punch holes in the top of their ornaments. String lengths of ribbon through the holes and tie the ends to make hangers. Allow children to make several sweet-smelling ornaments.

CRAFTY TIPS

✔ Make extra sandpaper shapes and let children decorate a classroom Christmas tree.

✔ Children may tie lengths of ribbon around cinnamon sticks to make another kind of scented ornament.

EXTRA FUN

This fun game lets children decorate moving trees!

Choose one child to be the Tree and give the other children each an ornament. Have the Tree twirl and tiptoe around the room with outstretched hands. Encourage the other children to try to hang their ornaments on the "branches" of the Tree. For a festive mood, play upbeat Christmas music and watch the children enjoy the celebration of decoration. Continue until each child is "decked out" for the holidays.

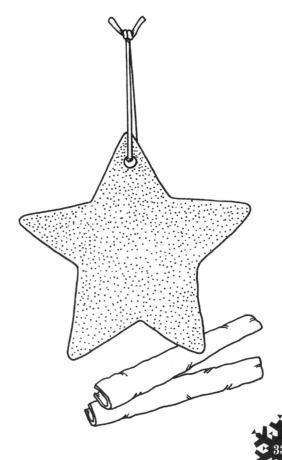

Jingle-Bell Bracelets

CRAFTY TIPS

✔ Let children make bells for their ankles then march around the room in a jingle-bell parade!

✔ Play Jingle-Bell Ponies! When you jingle your bell, have children trot like ponies on one-horse open sleighs! When you say, "Whoa!" have ponies stop.

SIMPLE SUPPLIES

You'll need large jingle bells and 8-inch lengths of red ribbon.

DIRECTIONS

❶ Give each child a large jingle bell and an 8-inch piece of red ribbon.

❷ Help children thread the ribbons through the loop on the bells. Show them how to hold both ends of the ribbon with the bell hanging down. Help each child tie the ribbon to keep the bell in the middle.

❸ Gently tie a Jingle-Bell Bracelet to each child's wrist.

EXTRA FUN

Let children try out their new Jingle-Bell Bracelets while singing this song to the tune of (what else?) "Jingle Bells."

Holy Lord, Holy Lord—
That's what my bells say! *(Hold up bracelet.)*
I'm so glad our Holy Lord *(point to face and smile)*
Was born on Christmas Day! *(Shake bracelet.)*

Holy Lord, Holy Lord—
That's what my bells say! *(Hold up bracelet.)*
I'm so glad our Holy Lord *(point to face and smile)*
Was born on Christmas Day! *(Shake bracelet.)*

Snowflake Sparkles

SIMPLE SUPPLIES

You'll need notched craft sticks, scissors, cups of tacky craft glue, cotton swabs, glitter glue in a variety of colors, tape, yarn, and wax paper.

DIRECTIONS

❶ Before class cut the yarn into 6-inch pieces.

❷ Cover a table with wax paper. Tape the paper's edges under the table to hold them in place. Set out the craft glue, glitter glue, cotton swabs, and yarn.

❸ Give each child three or four craft sticks. Help children tie a piece of yarn to the middle of one of the sticks.

❹ Show children how to glue the sticks in the shape of a snowflake by dipping the cotton swabs in glue, placing a small dab of glue on the middle of each stick, and stacking the sticks.

❺ Encourage children to decorate their snowflakes with the colorful glitter glue. Set the snowflakes aside to dry.

When the snowflakes are dry, let children dangle their sparkly creations while saying this little rhyme.

EXTRA FUN

Snowflakes fall upon my face.
I see snowflakes every place.
Sparkle down in winter sun—
So much fun for everyone!

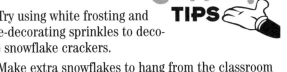
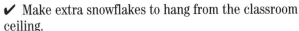

CRAFTY TIPS

✔ Try using white frosting and cake-decorating sprinkles to decorate snowflake crackers.

✔ Make extra snowflakes to hang from the classroom ceiling.

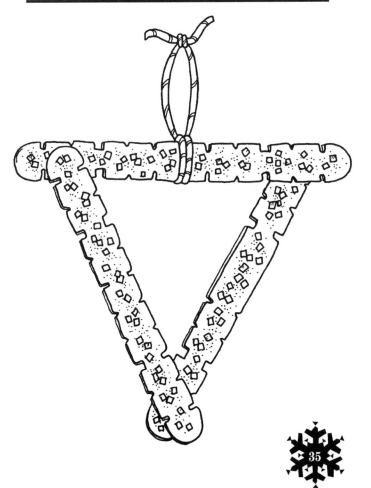

Edible Snowmen

CRAFTY TIPS

✔ Let children make snow-balls and form them into a fun snow fort, an igloo, or another cold creation.

✔ Make a large supply of edible snowballs and take them to a nearby children's home to brighten the residents' winter days.

SIMPLE SUPPLIES

You will need a batch of marshmallow and crisp rice cereal treat mix, a bowl of water, a measuring cup, white frosting, candy corn, button candies, raisins, licorice whips, flaked coconut (optional), paper plates, plastic knives, tape, and wax paper.

DIRECTIONS

❶ Before class prepare the marshmallow and crisp rice cereal recipe. Cover tables with wax paper. Tape the ends under the table to keep them from slipping.

❷ Give each child a paper plate and about ½ cup of the cereal mixture. Have children wet their hands in the bowl of water to keep the mixture from sticking to their fingers.

❸ Encourage children to make one large, one medium, and one small ball. If using coconut, place the coconut in a bowl and invite children to roll the "snowballs" in it.

❹ Invite the children to spread a small amount of the frosting to glue candy-corn noses, button-candy eyes, raisin buttons, and licorice-whip scarves onto their snowmen.

Let children use their snowmen in this counting rhyme.

EXTRA FUN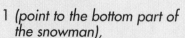

1 *(point to the bottom part of the snowman),*
2 *(point to the middle part of the snowman),*
3 *(point to the snowman's head)—*
Snowman play with me!

3 *(point to the snowman's head),*
2 *(point to the middle part of the snowman),*
1 *(point to the bottom part of the snowman)—*
He's melting in the sun.

"He gives a command to the earth, and it quickly obeys him. He spreads the snow like wool… Then he gives a command, and it melts" (Psalm 147:15-18).

Stuffy Snowmen

SIMPLE SUPPLIES

You'll need men's white socks, ½-inch pompons, triangles of orange felt, rubber bands, 10-inch pieces of ribbon, black construction paper, a hole punch, glue, and fiberfill.

DIRECTIONS

1 Set out fiberfill. Give each child one sock and have the children push fiberfill into their socks, filling them up to the cuff lines.

2 Give each child two rubber bands. Help each child fasten a rubber band around the sock cuff.

3 Show children how to make a snowman's head by placing a rubber band around the heel of the sock. Children may need some help securing the rubber bands with the correct tension.

4 Instruct children to tie the piece of ribbon just below the head as a scarf, covering the rubber band.

5 Show the children how to turn the cuff of the sock down over the head, then roll about 1 inch up to form a cute ski cap. Let children glue pompons on top of the ski caps.

6 Have children dab glue on the back of the "carrot noses" and press them onto the center of the heads.

7 Have children use a hole punch to make black construction paper dots to glue on for eyes, mouths, and buttons.

EXTRA FUN

After the glue is set, give children their snowmen and lead them in singing this song to the tune of "I'm a Little Tea-Pot."

I have a little snowman *(hold snowman up)*,
See him hop! *(Gently bounce snowman.)*
Look at his buttons *(point to buttons)*
And his hat on top. *(Point to hat.)*
I can hug my snowman. *(Hug snowman.)*
We play all day. *(Twirl around with snowman.)*
And he won't ever melt away! *(Hold snowman up.)*

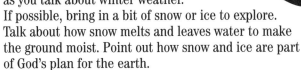

CRAFTY TIPS

✔ Use these plump snowmen as you talk about winter weather. If possible, bring in a bit of snow or ice to explore. Talk about how snow melts and leaves water to make the ground moist. Point out how snow and ice are part of God's plan for the earth.

✔ These snowy characters will amaze you with their unique qualities. Encourage children to name their snowmen and tell you about them. Stuffy Snowmen are great to use during lessons on individual uniqueness.

Pine Cone Bird Feeders

CRAFTY TIPS

✔ If pine cones are not available, use bread. Poke a small hole through the corner of a fresh slice of bread, allow it to dry, then loop string through the hole. Then spread the bread with peanut butter and press it in birdseed.

✔ Pine Cone Bird Feeders make wonderful gifts for grandparents and other relatives. Don't wait for a special holiday or event—just give them as gifts of love!

SIMPLE SUPPLIES

You'll need pine cones, peanut butter, craft sticks, birdseed, string or yarn, pie pans, small plastic bags, and damp washcloths.

DIRECTIONS

❶ Before class wrap and tie string around the smaller end of each pine cone and knot the ends to make a loop for hanging.

❷ Set out separate pie pans of peanut butter and birdseed. Give each child a pine cone on a string and a craft stick. Show children how to spread peanut butter on their pine cones.

❸ Then have children roll their pine cones in the pan of birdseed. Encourage children to press the pine cones into the birdseed firmly to make the seeds stick.

❹ Slide finished bird feeders into plastic bags to keep the seeds intact. Tell children to have their parents remove the plastic bag and help tie the string to a tree branch at home.

❺ Wash sticky hands with damp washcloths.

EXTRA FUN

Have children hold their bird feeders in one hand while pretending the other hand is a flighty bird coming for snacks. Then say this "tweet" rhyme.

Little bird, fly here and eat. *(Bring hand, fluttering, down to feeder.)*
I have made a special treat. *(Pretend hand is a bird eating food.)*
Peanut butter, birdseed, too *(say "yum")*—
A special gift from me to you. *(Point to self then to feeder.)*
God loves you, and so do I. *(Point up to God and then to self.)*
I love to watch you in the sky. *("Fly" the hand up in the air.)*

Repeat the rhyme and invite children to be pretend birds.

Soapy Snowballs

SIMPLE SUPPLIES

You'll need wax paper, tape, soap flakes such as Ivory Snow, a large mixing bowl, a measuring cup, vanilla flavoring, water, plastic sandwich bags, and ribbon.

DIRECTIONS

❶ Before class cover a table with wax paper. Tape the edges under the table to keep them from slipping.

❷ Have children help you measure 4 cups of soap flakes into a large bowl and add ¼ cup of water and a dash of vanilla flavoring.

❸ Let children take turns kneading the mixture. Add more water or soap flakes as needed to make a dough that will hold its shape. CAUTION: Warn children not to rub their eyes until they've rinsed the soap dough off their hands.

❹ Divide the dough among the children and show them how to form soapy snowballs.

❺ Let the dough dry for several minutes, then help children put their soapy snowballs into sandwich bags and tie the bags with ribbons.

EXTRA FUN

Explain that the Bible tells us that Jesus can take away all the bad things we've done and make us all clean inside. Then let preschoolers have a cleaning spree in your room. Provide dust cloths, paper towels, and spray bottles of mild glass-cleaner. Let children clean to their hearts' delight. Then talk about how nice it is to have a sparkling clean room and how good it feels on the inside when Jesus takes away our sins and makes us new and clean.

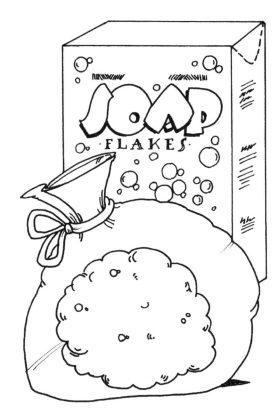

"We all have different gifts, each of which came because of the grace God gave us" (Romans 12:6a).

Let It Snow

CRAFTY TIPS

✔ Let children glue their snowflakes on a bulletin board with a dark blue background. Title the display "Let It Snow!" or "Each One Is Special!"

✔ Use wrapping-paper circles for fancy snowflake designs. Hang the snowflakes from coat hangers to make frosty mobiles.

SIMPLE SUPPLIES

You'll need scissors and 8-inch paper circles.

DIRECTIONS

❶ Before class cut thin paper into 8-inch circles. Cut two circles for each child. Cake-pan liners work well for this activity. (Hint: Coffee filters will *not* work well for this project—they're difficult to tear.)

❷ Help children fold the circles in half, then in half again, and once more to form pie shapes. Assure children that the folds don't need to be exact.

❸ Let children use their imaginations and muscles to tear small bits from the three sides of their pie shapes. Have children tear as many holes as they like, but be sure the holes don't touch each other.

❹ When children are finished tearing the holes, have them open the paper circles to see the beautiful, snowy designs and patterns.

EXTRA FUN

Have children hold their paper snowflakes in the air and look at them. Point out that the pattern of each snowflake is different from the others, just as God made each of us different. Then sing this active song to the tune of "Eency Weency Spider." Let children toss their snowflakes in the air to make a blizzard!

One little snowflake fell from up above. (Holding your snowflakes, pretend to let one float to the ground.)
Then came a second flake, white just like a dove. (Pretend to let the second snowflake float to the ground.)
When the ground was covered ("float" the snowflakes back and forth, showing snow-covered ground),
The children pranced with glee. ("Dance" the snowflakes back and forth.)
Each little snowflake's special (continue moving snowflakes)—
Just like you 'n' me! (Put snowflakes over your heart.)

Sleeping-Bear Puppets

SIMPLE SUPPLIES

You'll need tacky craft glue, scissors, craft sticks, paper cups, brown construction paper, black markers, and brown crayons.

DIRECTIONS

❶ Before class cut a slit in the bottom of each paper cup. Cut small, brown construction paper triangles to make pairs of ears. Be sure to prepare a paper cup and a pair of paper ears for each child.

❷ Set out crayons, markers, glue, and craft sticks. Hand each child a craft stick and have children color the sticks brown.

❸ Let children use black markers to draw eyes and noses on the top portions of the craft sticks to make bears. Then hand each child a pair of paper ears to glue on the top of the craft stick.

❹ Distribute the paper cups and have children color the cups brown. Help children insert the craft-stick "bears" through the slits in the bottoms of the cups. Let children practice moving their bears into the "caves" for a nap.

Remind children that God gives us places to live and grow. Explain that bears live in caves. Invite children to put their bears to bed then wake them up again in this fun action rhyme.

EXTRA FUN

God made homes for everyone *(wiggle the bear puppet),*
Even Mr. Bear. *(Make the puppet bow.)*
He goes deep inside his den *(move the puppet into the cup)*
While it's cold out there.
Quiet now, beside his cave *(place your finger on your lips),*
Hush! Don't make a sound!
We don't want to wake him up *(shake head "no")*
Before spring comes around.
Oh no! I think he's waking up *(make puppet peek out of cup),*
And when he does, watch out.
He might come out of his dark den *(poke the puppet out of the cup)*
With a growl or snort or shout! *(Make growling noises.)*

CRAFTY TIPS

✔ Use this same idea to make birds in nests, butterflies in cocoons, or groundhogs in their holes. This makes a great craft project to use when learning about God's provision.

✔ Use the bear puppets to play a fun game of Peekaboo with young toddlers or preschoolers.

Tricky Tracks

CRAFTY TIPS

✔ Add a few drops of food coloring to the shaving cream to make colorful, whimsical tracks.

✔ Try using sandpaper instead of construction paper to make textured trail tracks.

SIMPLE SUPPLIES

You'll need shaving cream, paint shirts, empty spools of thread, craft sticks, plastic spoons, and black or blue construction paper.

DIRECTIONS

❶ Set out cans of shaving cream, empty spools, craft sticks, plastic spoons, and construction paper.

❷ Have children wear paint shirts or paper grocery sacks with holes cut out for heads and arms. Let each child squirt a golf-ball-sized blob of shaving cream on the table top. Tell children that it's pretend snow but not to get the snow in their eyes or mouths. (Shaving cream is nontoxic but tastes icky!)

❸ Encourage children to make designs and tracks in the snow using spools, spoons, craft sticks, and their fingers.

❹ When the designs are finished, carefully place a sheet of construction paper over each design, gently smooth the paper down, then carefully lift the paper off the table.

EXTRA FUN

While the Tricky Tracks are drying, take your children on a trail of fun around the classroom. Tape paper footprints on the floor in a circle and play this game.

Tell the children that they may begin walking around the circle of footprints. Play lively background music. Explain that when you say, "Tricky-track trail," everyone should turn to go the other way. Continue playing until all the "trail hands" are ready for a treat. Have cookies shaped like big feet ready for the end of the trail.

Rainbows in January

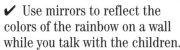
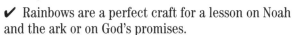

✔ Use mirrors to reflect the colors of the rainbow on a wall while you talk with the children.

✔ Rainbows are a perfect craft for a lesson on Noah and the ark or on God's promises.

SIMPLE SUPPLIES

You'll need wire coat hangers; yarn; scissors; tape; and red, orange, yellow, green, blue, and purple construction paper.

DIRECTIONS

❶ Before class cut a pile of colored construction paper into 5-inch squares. Cut six 6-inch pieces of yarn for each child.

❷ Give each child a square of each color of paper. Show children how to roll and tape their paper squares into mini-tubes.

❸ Hand six pieces of yarn to each child. Have children tape yarn to the tubes then tape the hanging tubes to coat hangers to create rainbow mobiles. Be sure each child has all the different colors of the rainbow hanging from his or her mobile.

Let children point to the colors of their rainbow mobiles as you say this rhyme together.

EXTRA FUN

Red, yellow, orange so bright,
Shining here against the light.
Green and purple and pretty blue—
God made rainbows for me and you!

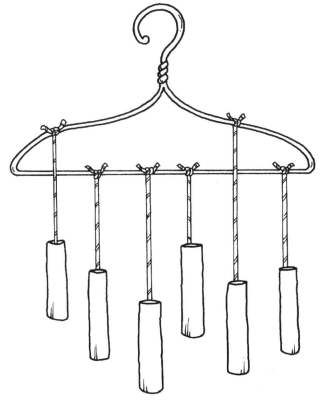

"It is written in the Scriptures: 'You must worship the Lord your God and serve only him'" (Luke 4:8).

Church Windows

 **TIPS**

✔ Church Windows are a nice addition to lessons on Solomon's Temple.

✔ Children may want to illustrate a Bible story on their vinyl squares.

✔ Rubbing alcohol will remove any permanent marker that is drawn on the tables during this craft.

SIMPLE SUPPLIES

You'll need clear, non-adhesive vinyl; scissors; several colors of permanent markers; newspaper; and paint shirts.

DIRECTIONS

❶ Before class cut a 6-inch square of clear, non-adhesive vinyl for each child. (Clear, non-adhesive vinyl is available at fabric or craft stores.)

❷ Cover a table with newspaper. To protect their clothing, help children put on paint shirts or paper grocery sacks with holes cut out for heads and arms.

❸ Hand each child a square of vinyl. Have children use permanent markers to color one side of the vinyl squares. Supervise children closely to prevent marker ink from staining their hands or clothes.

❹ When children have completed their Church Windows, show them how to press the clean side of the vinyl against a glass window. The static electricity created between the vinyl and the window will hold the colorful creations in place.

EXTRA FUN

Explain that many churches have pretty stained glass windows. Point out how pretty the windows look when the sun shines through them. Tell children that when we're kind to others, God's love shines through us.

Sing the following song to the tune of "Are You Sleeping?" Encourage children to hold their windows up to the light and peek through them.

My church windows,
My church windows—
Sun shines through.
Sun shines through.
We are like the windows.
We are like the windows.
God shines through.
God shines through.

Snow Art

SIMPLE SUPPLIES

You'll need spray bottles of colored water and a snowy day.

DIRECTIONS

❶ Before class fill spray bottles with water and add three drops of food coloring to each one. Make a variety of colors.

❷ Bundle everyone up and go outside. Find an area where the snow is smooth and fresh.

❸ Give children the spray bottles and let them "paint" pictures by spraying colored water on the snow.

❹ Form a long line and have children pass the spray bottles after each squirt. Encourage children to work together to make snow flowers, stars, or angels. Let them tell you about their creations.

❺ Make the outing brief to avoid chills and spills!

EXTRA FUN

Lead children on a tour of the snow paintings. Preschoolers will enjoy pointing out the colors they used to make their snow murals. Encourage children to tell about their paintings and how they made them.

As you tour the paintings, take small steps in the snow and challenge preschoolers to step only in your footsteps. Talk about how Jesus wants us to follow his footsteps.

CRAFTY TIPS

✔ Let children make snowballs with "painted" snow. Gather the snowballs in a plastic resealable bag, then place them in a freezer. Surprise children with snowy fun on a hot summer day when no snow is in sight—and explain that all things are possible with God!

Sticky Friends

CRAFTY TIPS

✔ To eliminate sticky goo on fingers, let children rub a bit of lemon juice on their hands and fingers then wipe them with damp paper towels.

SIMPLE SUPPLIES

You'll need popcorn, honey, scissors, a large mixing bowl, wax paper, vegetable oil, wet wipes, and gift-wrap ribbon or yarn. You'll also need access to a hot-air popcorn popper or hot water.

DIRECTIONS

❶ Before class cut ribbon or yarn into 8-inch lengths. You'll need one 8-inch length for each child.

❷ Cover your work area with wax paper. Tape the edges under the table to keep them from slipping.

❸ Make popcorn with the hot-air popper, put the popcorn in a large mixing bowl, then drizzle honey over the freshly popped popcorn. (If you have to make the popcorn before class, warm the honey by placing the jar of honey in hot water. Then drizzle the warmed honey over the popcorn.) Mix the honey and the popcorn together.

❹ Drop a mound of the mixture on a piece of wax paper for each child. Help children rub a drop of vegetable oil on their hands before molding the sticky popcorn.

❺ Have children shape the mixture into fun shapes or creatures. Allow each child to make two sticky shapes—one to keep and one to give to a friend.

❻ Place the snack that's for a friend on a piece of wax paper, gather the corners and edges up, then tie the gift with colorful ribbon or yarn. Set the wrapped popcorn balls aside for children to take home. Invite children to eat and enjoy their sticky treats after playing the Extra Fun game.

EXTRA FUN

Play a hopping game of Sticky Friends. Have children jump and hop, pretending to be popcorn. Encourage them to look for other popcorn to stick to by linking arms, holding hands, or putting a hand on each other's shoulder or around the waist. Have them pop around, touching others, sticking together until everyone ends up in one big popcorn ball. Play the game several times, then encourage children to sit together with a friend and eat the popcorn balls they made earlier.

Follow-Me Paintings

SIMPLE SUPPLIES

You'll need newspaper, paint shirts, paper cups, construction paper, a shoe box with the lid, tempera paint, large marbles, and plastic spoons.

DIRECTIONS

❶ Before class pour colored tempera paint into paper cups. Add two marbles and a plastic spoon to each cup. Cut or fold pieces of construction paper to fit inside the bottom of the box and lid. You'll need two pieces of paper for each child.

❷ Cover a table with newspaper. Set out the paint, the box and lid, and the paper.

❸ Have children put on paint shirts or grocery sacks with holes cut out for heads and arms.

❹ Demonstrate how to place a sheet of paper inside the box or lid. Help children use the plastic spoons to scoop the marbles out of the paint cups then place the marbles on the papers in the box or lid.

❺ Invite children to carefully tip the box from side to side so the marbles roll back and forth across the paper. Point out how the paint follows the marbles around and around the box. Help children put the marbles back into the paint cups to use again. Encourage children to use a variety of colors for their pictures.

CRAFTY TIPS

✔ Cover the pictures with clear, self-adhesive paper to create beautiful place mats for children to take home.

✔ For a great effect, try using golf balls instead of or in addition to the marbles.

EXTRA FUN

Remind children that we follow Jesus in many ways such as being helpful, talking nicely, and showing love to others. As the pictures dry, let children lie on their sides and pretend to be marbles as they roll around the floor and repeat this action rhyme.

> 'Round and 'round and 'round I roll
> Each and every day.
> 'Round and 'round and 'round I roll,
> Following Jesus all the way!

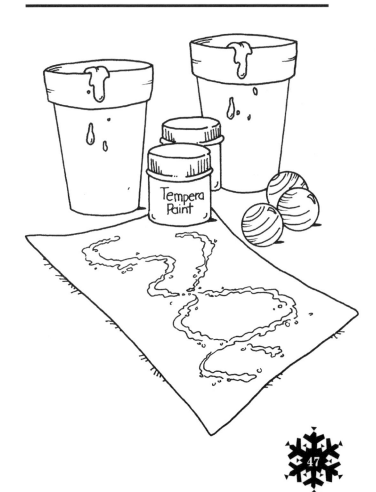

Gobbling Groundhogs

CRAFTY TIPS

✔ Take children on a walk outside to see their shadows. If they don't see them, could spring be right around the corner?

✔ Use this edible art activity to talk about God's animals: how they live, what they eat, and what "jobs" they perform.

✔ Use a similar cupcake idea at other times of the year: a bunny in its hole, a Christmas tree, or a bear emerging from its cave in spring.

SIMPLE SUPPLIES

You'll need one chocolate cupcake for each child, white icing, club crackers, chocolate chips and sprinkles for decoration, and plastic knives or craft sticks to spread the icing.

DIRECTIONS

❶ Set out icing, crackers, chocolate chips and sprinkles, and plastic knives or craft sticks.

❷ Hand each child a chocolate cupcake. Invite children to frost their cupcakes. Explain that it's like covering the ground with snow.

❸ Show children how to frost and decorate their crackers to look like groundhogs. Encourage them to make eyes and ears with little sprinkles and mouths with chocolate chips.

❹ Help children gently push the crackers into the top of their cupcakes to form groundhogs peeking out of the snow. Have extra crackers available in case of cracker crack-ups.

EXTRA FUN

This is a great time to play with shadows. Turn off the classroom lights and use a flashlight to shine on a white wall. Have children hold their cupcakes and make shadows with them.

Before they eat their treats, let children hold their groundhogs and share this rhyme.

> Winter days, often dark and cool—
> Play inside; that's the rule.
> I long to run outside and play
> With sunshine bright each and every day.
> But shadows fall across the snow,
> Yet spring is coming; this I know.
> God above tells me so!

Shadow Shapes

SIMPLE SUPPLIES

You'll need black construction paper, scissors, tape, and white chalk.

DIRECTIONS

❶ Before class cut 3×12-inch strips of black construction paper or black crepe paper. Cut two strips for each child.

❷ Hand each child two strips of black paper and a sheet of black construction paper. Show children how to tape the paper strips on the bottoms of their papers as legs.

❸ Invite children to use white chalk to add funny faces and any other details they'd like their "shadows" to have.

❹ Tape the paper legs to the back of each child's shoes to make his or her shadow. Encourage children to take their shadows for walks—and tell them to be careful not to step on someone else's shadow!

EXTRA FUN

Let children wear their shadows as you repeat the following action rhyme. Remind children to be careful not to step on other people's shadows!

Tiptoe, tiptoe *(tiptoe around the room)*,
Me and my shadow. *(Point to yourself.)*
Having fun wherever we go *(turn in a circle)*,
Me and my shadow. *(Point to yourself.)*

Hip-hop, hip-hop *(hop up and down)*,
Me and my shadow. *(Point to yourself.)*
Having fun wherever we go *(turn in a circle)*,
Me and my shadow. *(Point to yourself.)*

Let children suggest other actions such as
● jump up, jump down;
● twirl around; or
● back and forth.

CRAFTY TIPS

✔ Read Robert Louis Stevenson's classic poem "My Shadow." Talk about the fact that Jesus is always with us just as shadows follow us.

✔ Hang an old bedsheet as a backdrop, then let children use flashlights to give funny shadow shows!

Heart Wrapping-Paper

CRAFTY TIPS

✔ Very young preschoolers can sponge-paint first, then put stickers on their wrapping paper.

SIMPLE SUPPLIES

You'll need a roll of craft paper or white shelf paper (about 18 inches per child), heart stickers, tape, red or pink tempera paint, pie pans, newspaper, damp sponges, and paint shirts.

DIRECTIONS

❶ Before class pour tempera paint into shallow pie pans. Place a damp sponge in each pan.

❷ Cover your work area with newspaper. Have children wear paint shirts or paper grocery sacks with holes cut out for arms and heads.

❸ Tape the craft paper in place on your work area. Have the children place heart stickers randomly on the paper. Instruct children to gently press them down because they will peel the stickers off later.

❹ Let children sponge-paint over each sticker. Encourage children to paint the whole paper.

❺ Let the paint dry. You may speed the drying process with a blow-dryer or fan but use safety precautions with electrical equipment!

❻ Once the paint is partially dry, have children carefully peel off the stickers, revealing white hearts underneath. Leave in place any stickers that children can't readily remove from the paper. Cut a piece of "hearty paper" for each child to take home.

EXTRA FUN

Have children sit in a circle and hold their hearty papers. Let children take turns walking around the group while singing this song to the tune of "The Farmer in the Dell."

We're thankful for our friends;
We're thankful for our friends.
(Name) is walking 'round to show
(She's) thankful for (her) friends.

Play until each child has carried his or her hearty paper around the circle.

"God does not see the same way people see. People look at the outside of a person, but the Lord looks at the heart"
(1 Samuel 16:7b).

Heart Frames

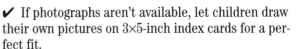

✔ Take pictures of children a few weeks ahead of time or use an instant camera for instant smiles.

✔ If photographs aren't available, let children draw their own pictures on 3×5-inch index cards for a perfect fit.

SIMPLE SUPPLIES

You'll need red poster board, a photograph of each child, crayons, scissors, glue sticks, a hole punch, and ribbon or yarn.

DIRECTIONS

❶ Before class cut red poster board into two 10×8-inch heart shapes for each child. Cut a 3×5-inch heart shape out of the middle of half of them.

❷ Set out glue sticks and crayons. Give each child two heart shapes—one solid and one with the small heart cutout.

❸ Show children how to place their photographs in the center of the large heart. Help children glue their photos in place using glue sticks.

❹ Invite children to use glue sticks to glue around the outside edges of the large hearts. Then show children how to place the hearts with the cutouts over the large hearts to make picture frames.

❺ Help each child punch a hole in the top of his or her heart then string ribbon or yarn through the hole. Knot the ribbons for the children to complete their heart frames.

❻ If there's time, allow children to decorate their frames with crayons or markers.

EXTRA FUN

Let children use their heart frames to play this twist on Hide-and-Seek.

Choose one child to be the first to hide his or her heart frame while the rest of the children close their eyes. Once the child has hidden the frame, have him or her say, "My heart is hidden away. Can you find it today?" Encourage children to look for the frame and cover their own hearts when they find it. Continue playing until everyone has had a chance to hide his or her heart.

Celebrate the "heart homecoming" with tasty treats. Make little sandwiches in heart-shaped cutouts.

"You made me and formed me with your hands" (Psalm 119:73a).

Self-Portrait Pizzas

CRAFTY TIPS

✔ This edible art idea is a warm illustration of God's unique creativity displayed in each child—and in each pizza.

✔ Plan this art activity with a party theme. Make the pizzas first, then play games while someone monitors the baking. After the pizzas cool, celebrate the uniqueness of each pizza and person.

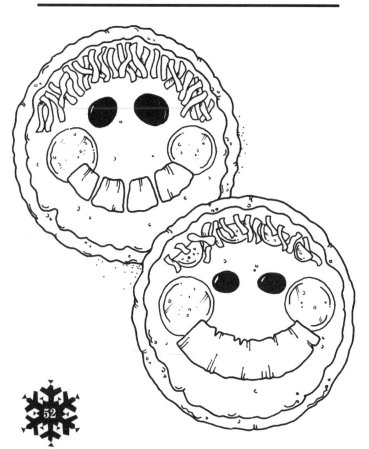

SIMPLE SUPPLIES

You'll need English muffins, pizza sauce, cheddar and mozzarella cheeses, olives, mushrooms, pineapple tidbits, pepperoni, other toppings as desired, bowls, plastic spoons, a cookie sheet, paint shirts, paper plates, and napkins. You'll also need access to a toaster oven or church oven.

DIRECTIONS

❶ Before class separate muffins into halves. Set out bowls of sauce, cheeses, and toppings with plastic spoons in each bowl. Let children wear paint shirts or paper grocery sacks with holes cut out for arms and heads.

❷ Have each child spread a spoonful of pizza sauce on half of an English muffin. Encourage children to add toppings to make faces on their muffins. Suggest using black olives for eyes, pineapple tidbits for mouths, and cheese for hair.

❸ When children have finished making their pizza faces, place them on a cookie sheet. Bake the pizzas until the cheese is melted and bubbly. Remove the pizzas from the oven and allow them to cool before giving them to the children to enjoy.

EXTRA FUN

While the pizzas are baking, teach the children this fun action poem.

God made my face *(point to face),*
My feet, my hands. *(Point to feet, hands.)*
I have a place *(point to self)*
In God's great plans. *(Hold hands wide.)*

When the pizzas are ready to eat, place them on paper plates. Have children walk around the table as they sing this song to the tune of "London Bridge."

God made me and all of you *(point to self, then others),*
All of you,
All of you.
God made me and all of you. *(Point to self, then others.)*
We are precious. *(Hug self.)*

Let's all eat our pizzas now *(point to pizzas),*
Pizzas now,
Pizzas now.
Let's all eat our pizzas now. *(Point to pizzas.)*
They look yummy. *(Rub tummy.)*
Umm!

PART 3

Spring Specials

Wind Paintings

CRAFTY TIPS

✔ Use poster board for larger Wind Paintings. Position one child on each side of the poster board and let the four children take turns blowing the paint.

✔ This activity works well with the story of the parting of the Red Sea. Place two puddles of red near the center of the paper about three inches apart and have the children blow the paint away from the center.

Tempera Paint

SIMPLE SUPPLIES

You'll need newspaper, tempera paint, water, small bowls, plastic spoons, coated paper such as shelf paper or finger paint paper, and paint shirts.

DIRECTIONS

❶ Before class thin several colors of tempera paint with water and place each color in a small bowl.

❷ Cover a table with newspaper and set out a sheet of coated paper for each child.

❸ Have children put on paint shirts or paper grocery sacks with holes cut out for arms and heads.

❹ Help children use plastic spoons to put a few small puddles of paint near the center of their papers, then let the blowing begin! Encourage children to pretend they're the March wind and to blow the colors out to the corners of their papers. Show children how to gently turn their papers to spread the paint as they blow.

EXTRA FUN

Try this lively action rhyme while you wait for the pictures to dry.

Whoosh! Whoosh!
    (Swing arms back and forth.)
The March wind blows. *(Keep swinging arms.)*
It blows over me *(point to self)*
From my head to my toes. *(Put hands on head, then touch toes.)*
Whoosh! Whoosh! *(Swing arms back and forth.)*
See the trees bend? *(Lean to one side.)*
God sends the wind *(point upward)*,
And God is my friend! *(Hug yourself.)*

Nesting Kites

SIMPLE SUPPLIES

You'll need plastic berry baskets or plastic needlepoint sheets; scissors; yarn; and any combination of the following: cotton balls, string, torn tissue paper, raffia, feathers, narrow ribbon, computer-paper side strips.

DIRECTIONS

❶ Before class cut the sides from the berry baskets or cut needlepoint sheets into 4×6-inch rectangles. Be sure to cut a rectangle for each child. Tie a 12-inch piece of yarn to one corner of each rectangle.

❷ Set out assorted craft items on the table. Let children choose at least four things to weave into the holes of their "kites."

❸ Help children weave the items in and out two or three times. Make sure items are woven in loosely enough so that birds are able to pull the items free.

❹ When children have finished weaving, explain that they can hang the nesting kites in trees near their homes. Birds will use the materials woven in the kites to make nests.

Invite children to "fly" their kites as you lead them in singing this song for our fine, feathered friends. Sing the song to the tune of "Mary Had a Little Lamb."

EXTRA FUN

Birdies, birdies take some string.
Take some string.
Take some string.
Birdies, birdies take some string.
To make a pretty nest!

Add other verses describing nesting items such as ribbon, cotton, or feathers.

CRAFTY TIPS

✔ Nesting Kites are a delightful addition to your springtime lessons and help spark great discussions about new life, taking care of others, and the birds on Noah's ark.

✔ Use this crafty idea to learn about God's provision and the homes we live in.

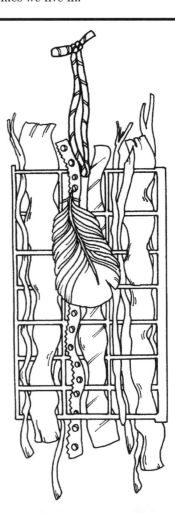

Lovely Lambs

CRAFTY TIPS

✔ This same craft idea can be used to make other animals such as puffy bunnies (add clothespin ears) or fuzzy polar bears.

✔ Use this lively little lamb while learning about the parable of the lost sheep.

SIMPLE SUPPLIES

You'll need cotton balls, white craft glue, scissors, a pie pan, cotton swabs, hinge-style clothespins, 3×5 index cards, black markers, and black construction paper.

DIRECTIONS

❶ Before class cut 3×5 index cards into oval shapes. You will need one oval for each child.

❷ Get out craft glue in a pie pan. Give each child a paper oval and a cotton swab. Have children use cotton swabs to spread glue on one side of their ovals.

❸ Give children cotton balls to glue on the ovals to make fluffy sheep.

❹ While the first side begins to dry, have children tear small scraps of black construction paper to make little lamb eyes, noses, and mouths. Let children glue faces on the cotton-covered sides of the ovals.

❺ Then have children turn the lambs over and glue cotton to the other side.

❻ Clip two clothespins on the bottom of each lamb to make four legs.

❼ Have children use black markers to color clip-clop hooves on the ends of the clothespins.

EXTRA FUN

Tell children the Bible tells us that Jesus is the good shepherd. Talk about how sheep follow the shepherd everywhere just as we follow Jesus. Say this little verse while children hold their own lovely little lambs.

As the shepherd knows his lambs *(pat little lamb)*,
God above knows who I am. *(Point up to heaven.)*
All I do or think or say *(point to self)*,
With love he guides me every day. *(Hug self.)*

Puffy Pussy Willows

SIMPLE SUPPLIES

You'll need 12×18-inch-sheets of construction paper, brown paper lunch bags, craft glue, glue sticks, paper cups, real or paper leaves, bowls, and popped popcorn.

DIRECTIONS

❶ Direct the children to rip brown paper lunch bags in strips to make the limbs of a tree.

❷ Set out glue sticks and construction paper. Have children glue the brown paper strips to sheets of construction paper so that the brown strips look like trees.

❸ Set out several cups of craft glue and bowls of popped popcorn. Show children how to dip popcorn in the glue and stick the popcorn to their paper branches. The popcorn will look like puffy pussy willows.

❹ Further embellish the pictures by gluing on real or paper leaves. Let each child munch a handful of popcorn as the pussy willows dry.

EXTRA FUN

Bring in a vase of pussy willows and let children feel their soft blossoms. Lead children in pretending to be blossoming plants. Begin by acting like a plant in the cold winter, then "blossom" as the weather gets warmer and warmer.

Say this pussy willow rhyme while the children hold their dried pussy willow pictures.

Puffy little pussy willows *(puff your cheeks and puff at your picture)*
On the branches bow. *(Bend your body to the right and left.)*
Puffy little pussy willows *(puff your cheeks and puff at your picture)*
Grow but don't meow! *(Say "meow.")*

CRAFTY TIPS

✔ For a Christmas variation of this craft idea, make green pine-tree shapes and decorate them with popcorn and Christmas decorations.

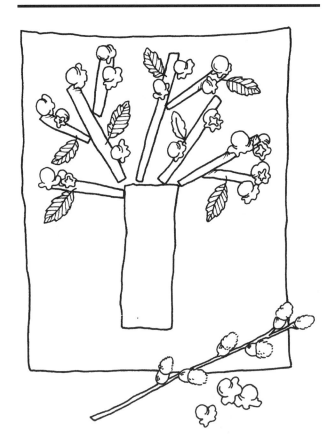

57

Cookie in a Bag

CRAFTY TIPS

✔ Cookie in a Bag works great with lessons about spices, such as the wise men or Jesus' friends bringing spices to his tomb.

SIMPLE SUPPLIES

You'll need small, resealable plastic bags; cinnamon-honey graham crackers; water; powdered sugar; measuring spoons; and napkins.

DIRECTIONS

❶ Give each child a resealable plastic bag and two graham crackers.

❷ Help children put the crackers in the bags then seal their bags. Let children crush the graham crackers into crumbs.

❸ Open the bags and add 1 teaspoon of water to each bag. Seal the bags and encourage the children to squish the dough in their bags until the dough forms into one lump.

❹ Open the bags and add ¼ teaspoon of powdered sugar to each bag. Seal the bags again and have children shake their cookies until they're coated with powdered sugar.

❺ Let children enjoy eating their cookies. The bags may be reused if each child would like to make another cookie.

EXTRA FUN

While the children are making their cookies, sing the following verses to the tune of **"If You're Happy and You Know It."**

Verse 1: If you're happy and you know it, make some crumbs.
If you're happy and you know it, make some crumbs.
If you're happy and you know it, then your face will surely show it.
If you're happy and you know it, make some crumbs.

Verse 2: If you're happy and you know it, make some dough.
Verse 3: If you're happy and you know it, shake, shake, shake.
Verse 4: If you're happy and you know it, give God thanks!

Come-Along Caterpillars

SIMPLE SUPPLIES

You'll need egg cartons, scissors, a hole punch, string, glue sticks, markers, and scraps of construction paper.

DIRECTIONS

❶ Before class remove each egg-carton lid and cut the cupped half into four equal parts. You will need one three-cup segment for each child.

Cut one 12-inch length of string for each child. Using a hole punch, make eyes from the construction paper scraps.

❷ Set out glue sticks, markers, and paper eyes. Hand each child an egg-carton section.

❸ Encourage children to decorate their caterpillars with markers. Tell children to glue on buggy eyes.

❹ Punch a hole at the front of each child's caterpillar and tie a string into the hole as a leash. Have children name their caterpillars.

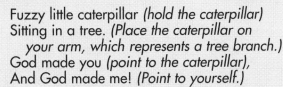

Teach children this fun rhyme while they act out the motions with their caterpillars.

EXTRA FUN

Fuzzy little caterpillar *(hold the caterpillar)*
Sitting in a tree. *(Place the caterpillar on your arm, which represents a tree branch.)*
God made you *(point to the caterpillar),*
And God made me! *(Point to yourself.)*

Fuzzy little caterpillar *(pat the caterpillar)*
Sitting in a tree. *(Place the caterpillar on your arm, which represents a tree branch.)*
Spin a warm cocoon *(turn in circles);*
We'll see what you will be. *(Hold hands up to eyes like binoculars.)*

CRAFTY TIPS

✔ Provide books and pictures of caterpillars, cocoons, and emerging butterflies during a lesson on change and growth.

✔ Use this craft idea with lessons about new life in Jesus.

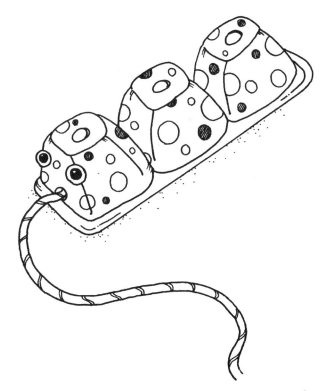

Cocoons and Butterflies

CRAFTY TIPS

✔ Host a spring-morning breakfast for parents. Serve doughnuts and juice. At each place, leave a surprise cocoon as a gift.

✔ Talk about our new life in Christ and how we become beautiful in him.

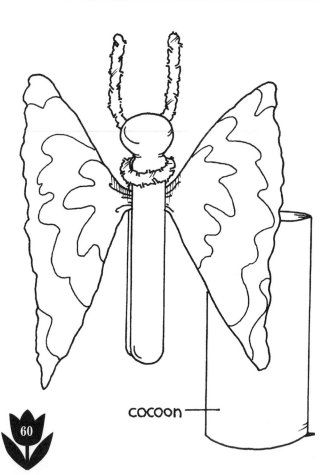

cocoon

SIMPLE SUPPLIES

You'll need coffee filters, scissors, newspaper, washable-ink markers, water, spray bottles, clothespins with round heads, tacky craft glue, black chenille wire, and empty bathroom-tissue tubes.

DIRECTIONS

❶ Before class cut chenille wire into a 4-inch length for each child.

❷ Cover the table with newspaper.

❸ Give each child a coffee filter. Encourage children to color their filters with colorful markers. Then show children how to lightly mist the filters with water.

❹ Set out tacky craft glue. Give each child a clothespin. Help put spots of glue on the inside of the clothespins.

❺ Gather the filters, then slide them into the clothespins. Arrange the wings of the newly formed "butterflies."

❻ Wrap chenille wires around the butterflies to create antennae.

❼ Push the butterflies inside the cardboard tubes. Let children gently pull the butterflies out of the "cocoons."

Use cocoon butterflies in this fun finger play.  **EXTRA FUN**

Once it was a wiggly worm
That crawled upon the ground. *(Wiggle your index finger.)*
Then one day I searched for it,
But it could not be found. *(Shake head.)*
I only found a little tube *(hold cocoon)*,
And I left it quite alone.
Mom said this had become
My caterpillar's home.

I waited for a long, long time.
I peeked in every day. *(Peek in cocoon tube.)*
I discovered his little home
No longer looked this way. *(Hold cocoon up.)*
His home had changed,
And in its place
I saw, with my own eyes,
A little shell
And my new friend—
Surprise! A butterfly! *(Push the butterfly out of its cocoon.)*

Colors of the Rainbow

SIMPLE SUPPLIES

You'll need newspaper, paint shirts, scissors, tempera paint, tape, paper cups, plastic spoons, and yarn. You'll also need two clear plastic plates for each child. (You can purchase clear plastic plates at party-supply or discount stores.)

DIRECTIONS

❶ Before class cut a 6-inch piece of yarn for each child.

❷ Cover a table with newspaper. Pour paint in paper cups and set them on the table.

❸ Have children put on paint shirts or paper grocery sacks with holes cut out for arms and heads.

❹ Give each child one clear plastic plate.

❺ Encourage children to decorate the centers of their plates with drips of different colors of paint.

❻ Give each child another clear plastic plate. Show children how to gently nest this plate over the painted one to squish the paint inside and stick the plates together.

❼ Help children tape the plates together around the edges. Tell children to make sure the plates stay together.

❽ Tape a yarn loop to the top of each plate so that the Colors of the Rainbow plate may be hung in a window to let the sun shine through the pretty colors.

EXTRA FUN

Have the children sit in a circle. Ask them to place their Colors of the Rainbow sun-catchers in the middle. Sing the following song to the tune of "Did You Ever See a Lassie?" Change the color of the rainbow in each verse and have children point to that color in their sun-catchers.

Did you ever see a rainbow, a rainbow, a rainbow?
Did you ever see a rainbow? A rainbow has red!
(Children point to the color red on their sun-catchers.)

Repeat this verse, changing the color named each time. Then repeat the song and have the children that are wearing each color stand up.

CRAFTY TIPS

✔ Colors of the Rainbow are a nice addition to lessons about springtime, Noah and the rainbow, or the diversity of God's creation.

✔ You may want to stir glitter into the tempera paint for a sparkling rainbow effect.

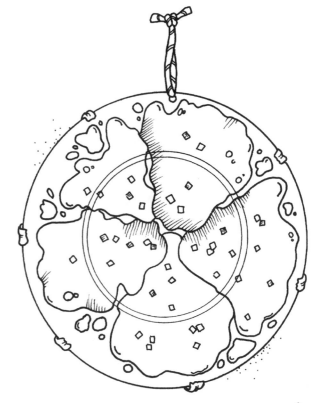

Waving in the Wind

CRAFTY TIPS

✔ Children can make smaller windsocks by using 1-inch widths cut from cardboard tubes. They can hang several of these from the bottom of a wire hanger.

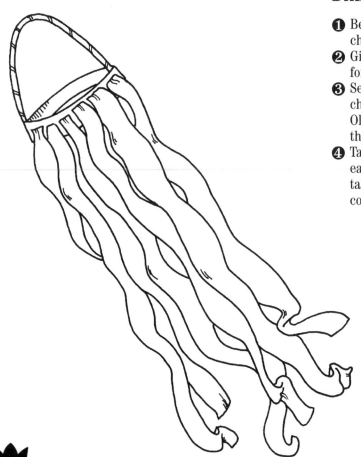

SIMPLE SUPPLIES

You'll need construction paper, crepe paper, scissors, yarn, and tape.

DIRECTIONS

❶ Before class cut a 2×11½-inch strip of construction paper and a 6-inch piece of yarn for each child. Cut several 12-inch crepe paper streamers for each child.

❷ Give each child a strip of construction paper and help him or her tape the two ends together to form a ring.

❸ Set out the crepe paper streamers and have children tape streamers around the rings. Older children may wish to tear the ends of the streamers for a fringed effect.

❹ Tape a piece of yarn on opposite sides of each ring to form a handle. Have children take their windsocks outside and watch the colorful streamers wave in the wind.

EXTRA FUN

Have children hold their windsocks up in the wind or wave them around if it's a still day. As they do, lead them in the following rhyming game.

Colors waving, blowing free.
What bright colors do you see?

Call on a child to tell a color that he or she sees. Repeat the rhyme so each child has a turn to play.

Eency Weency Spiders

SIMPLE SUPPLIES

You will need colored chenille wire, large colored pompons, tacky craft glue, a hole punch, construction paper, and scissors.

DIRECTIONS

❶ Before class cut chenille wire into 6-inch lengths. You'll need four pieces of wire for each child. Use a hole punch to make construction paper "eyes."

❷ Set out glue, pompons, and paper eyes. Give each child three pieces of wire. Have children hold the wires in one hand. Hand each child another wire. Show children how to wrap one chenille wire around the center of the other three then tuck in the ends to form the body of a spider.

❸ Have children glue large pompons on top of the wrapped chenille wires. Help children cover the top of the last wire with glue to keep the pompon in place.

❹ Let children glue paper eyes to their pompons.

❺ Help children bend the wire "spider legs" down so their spiders can "walk." Allow spiders to dry for 10 minutes before using them in the Extra Fun activity.

Children love to sing the song "Eency Weency Spider." Have them use their spiders to act out the song as you sing together.

The eency weency spider went up the water spout,
Down came the rain and washed the spider out,
Up came the sun and dried out all the rain,
So the eency weency spider went up the spout again.

✔ Tie strings to the spiders and take them for a spider stroll.

✔ Use Eency Weency Spiders with lessons on Creation to help children appreciate all that God created—even "creepy-crawlies."

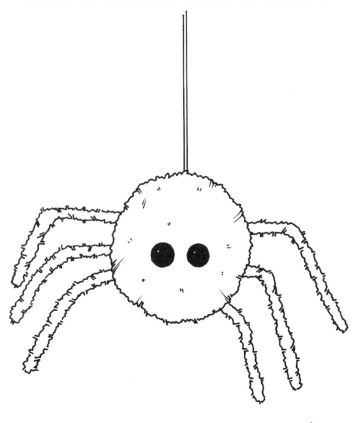

Drippity-Drop

CRAFTY TIPS

✔ Try using curling ribbon in place of the foil or tinsel. Cut hearts, raindrops, or cats and dogs from paper and tape them to the ends of the ribbons.

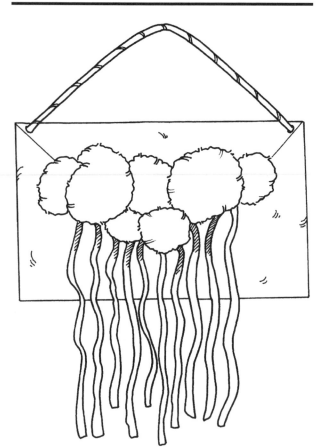

SIMPLE SUPPLIES

You'll need aluminum foil or tinsel, tape, cotton balls, glue, white envelopes, a hole punch, yarn, scissors, and paper towels.

DIRECTIONS

❶ Before class cut aluminum foil into ½×6-inch strips.

❷ Give each child an envelope and paper towel. Have children crumple the towels and stuff them into their envelopes to make clouds. Show children how to lick the envelope flaps and stick tinsel or foil "rain" on the adhesive before folding the flaps down. Tape any raindrops that won't stick.

❸ Have children glue cotton balls onto the sealed envelope flaps to make fluffy rain clouds.

❹ As each child finishes, punch holes at each end of the envelope top. String a length of yarn through the holes. Knot the ends of the yarn and let the child swirl the rain cloud through the air.

As children swirl their rain clouds, lead them in singing this rainy-day song to the tune of "The Farmer in the Dell."

EXTRA FUN

Drippity-drippa-drop,
Drippity-drippa-drop,
Rain is falling from the clouds.
I hope it never stops!

Squish-Paint Butterflies

SIMPLE SUPPLIES

You'll need paper plates, 3-inch lengths of chenille wire, tape, paint shirts, newspaper, several colors of tempera paint, plastic spoons, and plastic bowls.

DIRECTIONS

❶ Before class pour tempera paints into bowls. Place a plastic spoon in each bowl.

❷ Cover a table with newspaper and set out the paints. Have children wear paint shirts or grocery sacks with holes cut out for arms and heads.

❸ Give each child a paper plate. Demonstrate how to fold a plate in half. Be sure the children make good creases.

❹ Invite children to spoon a bit of paint onto one side of their plates then fold the plates. Encourage children to press gently on their plates, using their hands or fists.

❺ Let children open their paper plates to see the beautiful "butterflies" inside. Set the butterflies in the sun to dry for at least 15 minutes.

❻ When the "wings" are dry, give each child two pieces of chenille wire. Help children tape the chenille wires onto the tops of the butterflies as antennae.

Have children hold their colorful butterflies and flap the paper wings. Have them repeat the following rhyme as they "fly" their butterflies around the room.

Colors bright on floating wings,
It seems as if this creature sings!
From flower to flower it glides so high,
Flutter, flutter, butterfly!

CRAFTY TIPS

✔ Use this bright butterfly craft when you teach about new life in Jesus.

✔ Have the children make tactile butterflies using papers such as shelf paper, corrugated cardboard, or sandpaper.

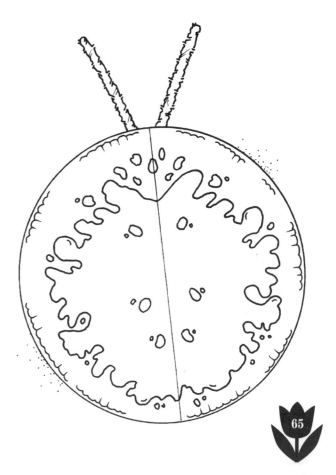

"Every seed will produce more of its own kind of plant" (Genesis 1:11b).

Spring Sprouts

CRAFTY TIPS

✔ Make a couple of Spring Sprouts as class projects and set them where the children can see the growth from week to week.

✔ Bring in a variety of seeds and nuts and invite children to taste them.

✔ Use this activity with a lesson about the parable of the sower and the seeds.

Kathy
May 16

SIMPLE SUPPLIES

You'll need dried beans such as lima or white beans, paper towels, resealable plastic bags, a bowl of water, masking tape, and a marker.

DIRECTIONS

❶ Prepare a sample sprout ahead of time. Show the green shoots and roots to the children so they will know what their sprouts will look like in a few days.

❷ Set out dried beans, paper towels, and a bowl of water. Help children dip their paper towels in the water then carefully wring out the excess water.

❸ Give each child a resealable plastic bag. Have children fold the towels to fit flat inside the bags.

❹ Invite children to select four or five dried beans, then place the beans on the damp paper towels inside their bags. Securely seal the bags.

❺ Label each bag with the child's name and date. Tell children to place their portable gardens in sunny windows. Encourage them to watch the roots and shoots as they begin to grow in the next two to three days.

EXTRA FUN

Visit with the children about what God provides to make things grow, such as sunshine, water, and good soil. Sing this song together to the tune of "Mary Had a Little Lamb" while doing the accompanying motions.

Little seed, so small and round *(curl up in a ball),*
Pushed way down into the ground.
With water and some sunshine glow *(begin to stretch up),*
God will help you grow—grow—GROW! *(Reach up higher and higher.)*

66

Flower Finger-Puppets

SIMPLE SUPPLIES

You'll need newspaper, scissors, cotton garden gloves, colorful markers, colored felt scraps, and tacky craft glue.

DIRECTIONS

1 Before class cut colored felt scraps into small, triangular petals. You'll also need to cut the fingers off of cotton garden gloves. You'll need one glove finger for each child.

2 Cover a table with newspaper. Set out bright markers, the felt flower petals, and tacky craft glue.

3 Hand each child a glove finger, then have children slip the glove fingers on. Invite children to color their glove fingers to look like bright flowers. Encourage children to color their fingertip portions yellow or pink and the rest of the glove fingers green.

4 Then let children glue felt petals around the fingertip portion to make flowers.

5 Help children use fine-tipped markers to draw eyes, noses, and smiling mouths on their flowers.

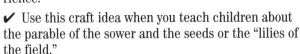

✔ Use rubber dish-washing gloves for a different tactile experience.

✔ Use this craft idea when you teach children about the parable of the sower and the seeds or the "lilies of the field."

Let children use their puppets as they sing this song to the tune of "Eency Weency Spider."

> Little spring flowers
> Sleep underground. *(Hide puppet under opposite hand.)*
> Shh—now peek and try to
> Find them all around. *(Look for other flowers.)*
> Soon you'll see
> A tiny little sprout *(show only the green knuckle between fingers of the opposite hand),*
> Then a tiny flower
> Will pop right out! *(Pop out your flower.)*

67

"In the same way, you should be a light for other people. Live so that they will see the good things you do and will praise your Father in heaven" (Matthew 5:16).

Mother's Day Candles

CRAFTY TIPS

✔ Have children present their candles to mommies or grandmas for special gifts.

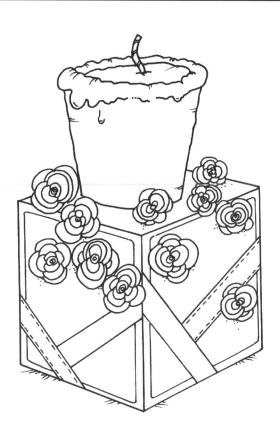

SIMPLE SUPPLIES

You'll need small wooden building blocks, ribbon, scissors, artificial rosebuds, tea-light candles, tacky craft glue, and a glue gun.

DIRECTIONS

❶ Before class cut 2-inch lengths of colorful ribbon.

❷ Set out craft glue, artificial rosebuds, and ribbon. Heat the glue gun away from the children and out of their reach.

❸ Give each child a wooden block. Let children glue rosebuds and colorful ribbon bits on four sides of the blocks to make pretty candleholders.

❹ Have adult helpers use the hot-glue gun to attach a tea-light candle to the top of each child's block. Set the candleholders aside to cool for at least 15 minutes.

Teach children this precious poem so they can say it when they give their candles to their mothers or other special people.

EXTRA FUN

This little candle shining bright
Shines for Jesus
And shows his light.
Like God's love,
It's bright and true.
And I made it
Just for you!

Crispy-Treat Flowers

SIMPLE SUPPLIES

You'll need a large glass bowl, 5½ cups of crisp rice cereal, 45 large marshmallows, ⅓ cup of margarine, large spoons, mini-muffin cups, colored sugar, and craft sticks. You'll also need access to a microwave oven.

DIRECTIONS

❶ Put the margarine in a large glass bowl and melt it in a microwave oven on high for 45 seconds. Add the marshmallows and toss them with the melted margarine. Microwave the mixture on high for one minute and 30 seconds or until the marshmallows are smooth when stirred.

❷ Let the children help you pour crisp rice cereal into the marshmallow mixture, then gently stir the treats.

❸ Help each child spread a bit of margarine in the mini-muffin cups. Then have children sprinkle colored sugar into the mini-muffin cups.

❹ Have the children take turns spooning some cereal mixture into their muffin cups. Fill each cup to the top.

❺ Help children insert craft sticks into the cereal mixture in the muffin cups to form stems. When the cereal mixture has cooled, help children carefully remove their Crispy-Treat Flowers from the mini-muffin cups.

Teach children this special thank you prayer before they gobble their treats.

EXTRA FUN

Thank you, Lord, for birds and bees.
Thank you for the flowers and trees.
Thank you for this special treat
And all the good things we can eat.

CRAFTY TIPS

✔ Have children each make two Crispy-Treat Flowers. Then form a yummy "bouquet" with the flowers and deliver the bouquet to another class.

✔ To create colorful flowers, add a bit of food coloring to your marshmallow mixture.

✔ Use nonstick spray to coat muffin tins before class.

Good and Fruity

CRAFTY TIPS

✔ Roll the dough into long ropes and line up the colors to make delicious rainbows.

SIMPLE SUPPLIES

You'll need powdered sugar, peanut butter, a plastic spoon, cupcake liners, and an airtight container.

DIRECTIONS

❶ Before class mix 2 cups of powdered sugar and ½ cup of peanut butter. Knead until the mixture forms a smooth dough. Store the dough in an airtight container.

❷ Have children wash their hands, then give each child a cupcake liner and a small portion of edible dough. Show children how to form fruits such as grapes, bananas, oranges, and apples.

❸ Encourage children to fill their cupcake-liner "bowls" with different fruits. Ask children to save one piece of fruit for the Extra Fun activity then enjoy gobbling up their other edible-dough fruit.

EXTRA FUN

Make a "Fruits of the Spirit" tree. Draw a tree on a large sheet of paper and tape it to a wall. Have the children sit in front of the tree on the floor. Invite each child to press a fruity shape onto the tree and tell what kind of fruit it is. Have children hold hands, form a circle, and sing the following song to the tune of "Here We Go 'Round the Mulberry Bush."

> The fruits of the Spirit are love, joy, peace,
> Love, joy, peace,
> Love, joy, peace.
> The fruits of the Spirit are love, joy, peace
> All through the day.

Baby Peeps

SIMPLE SUPPLIES

You'll need clay, paper sacks, plastic eggshell halves, cotton balls, tacky craft glue, construction paper, and nature items.

DIRECTIONS

❶ Give children paper sacks and let them walk outside looking for bird-nest materials such as small twigs, grasses, and small leaves. Tell the children to pretend that they're birds building nests.

❷ When you return to the classroom, give each child an apple-sized lump of clay. Encourage children to shape the clay into nests. Then show children how to press the nature items they gathered into their clay nests.

❸ Set out tacky glue. Give each child a plastic eggshell half and a cotton ball. Help children glue cotton-ball "chicks" inside the plastic eggshell halves. You may use real eggshell halves if you desire.

❹ Let children tear tiny construction paper eyes and beaks and then glue them to the cotton balls.

❺ Have children place their little chicks in their nests.

Let children gently hold their nests and baby birds as you repeat the following rhyme together.

EXTRA FUN

Peep, peep, baby bird. *(Gently cradle your "bird.")*
Jesus loves you, have you heard? *(Look upward, then put your ear to the bird as if you're listening to its peeps.)*

CRAFTY TIPS

✔ Baby peeps are a delightful addition to your springtime lessons and spark great discussions about new life during the Easter season.

✔ Use mud instead of clay for a different effect.

"Let's go early to the vineyards and see if the buds are on the vines. Let's see if the blossoms have already opened and if the pomegranates have bloomed" (Song of Solomon 7:12).

Buds and Blossoms

CRAFTY TIPS

✔ On Arbor Day talk about how trees and blooming flowers help our environment. Plant a class tree or rosebush.

✔ Substitute thumb prints for cereal blossoms by using a washable-ink pad.

✔ Silk flower buds found in craft-supply stores could be used on the tree branches instead of cereal.

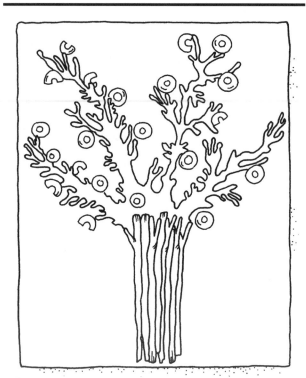

SIMPLE SUPPLIES

You'll need tempera paint, paint shirts, plastic spoons, straws, colorful cereal, white craft glue, pie pans, newspaper, and glossy paper such as white shelf paper or butcher paper.

DIRECTIONS

❶ Cover a table with newspaper. Set out pie pans with ½ inch of tempera paint and a plastic spoon in each one.

❷ Have children wear paint shirts or grocery sacks with holes cut out for arms and heads. Hand each child a large sheet of shelf paper.

❸ Let each child put a spoonful of paint near one edge of the paper. This is the trunk of the tree. For a different twist on the trunk, you may want to have children glue sandpaper strips or real twigs to their papers.

❹ Give each child a straw. Show children how to blow through the straws to make the paint spread out across their papers. Encourage them to keep blowing until they have enough "branches" for the trees.

❺ Set out glue and colorful cereal bits. Have children glue the cereal bits along the branches of the trees. Let pictures dry for 10 minutes.

EXTRA FUN

Sing this song to the tune of "Mary Had a Little Lamb" while you sway in the "breeze." Have children hold their blossoming tree pictures and make them sway as the children sing.

Trees are swaying in the breeze *(move your picture from side to side),*
In the breeze, in the breeze. *(Continue swaying.)*
Trees are swaying in the breeze *(continue swaying)*
On this bright spring day! *(Hold picture high above head.)*

Flowers bud upon the trees *(point to colorful cereal "buds"),*
Upon the trees, upon the trees. *(Continue pointing.)*
Flowers bud upon the trees *(continue pointing)*
On this bright spring day! *(Hold picture high above head.)*

Fields of Flowers

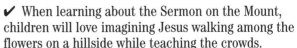

SIMPLE SUPPLIES

You'll need white craft glue, water, potpourri refresher oil, paintbrushes, blue and green construction paper, brightly colored tissue paper, a hole punch, straws, and several shallow boxes.

DIRECTIONS

1 Before class dilute white craft glue with water and add two or three drops of potpourri refresher oil. Use a hole punch to make lots of colorful dots of tissue paper. Place the tissue paper dots in the shallow boxes.

2 Set out the paintbrushes and scented glue. Give each child one sheet each of blue and green construction paper.

3 Show children how to tear the green construction paper in half horizontally. Then let children use the paintbrushes to glue the "green grass" on their blue sheets of construction paper.

4 Have children brush spots of glue on the green grass in their pictures.

5 Give each child a straw. Place the boxes with tissue paper dots on the table. Show children how to put a picture in a box with one hand and blow with a straw into the tissue. Pieces of tissue will fly onto the papers, creating a beautiful "field of flowers."

> **While the projects are drying, enjoy this fun finger rhyme.** **EXTRA FUN**
>
> God gave the flowers *(wiggle your fingers like flower petals)*
> A beautiful smell *(touch nose)*
> And beautiful colors to see. *(Touch eyes.)*
> Since God was so careful *(point up)*
> To take care of them,
> I know he'll take care of me! *(Point to self.)*

✔ For another fragrant possibility, try misting spray cologne on the Fields of Flowers pictures.

✔ When learning about the Sermon on the Mount, children will love imagining Jesus walking among the flowers on a hillside while teaching the crowds.

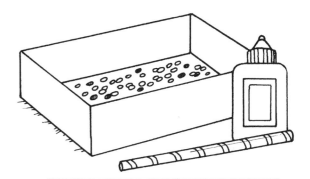

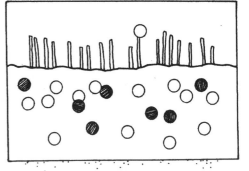

"Everyone who had blue, purple, and red thread, and fine linen... brought them to the Lord" (Exodus 35:23).

Springtime Flags

CRAFTY TIPS

✔ For an unusual effect, gather portions of the cloth and wrap rubber bands tightly around the gathers. Spray the gathered portions of cloth with colored water, then remove the rubber bands after the fabric dries.

✔ Allow children to place several strips of masking tape across the cloth before spraying it. Pull the tape off after the cloth dries to discover a creative design.

✔ Do not wash your colored fabrics! The food color will fade and may completely wash out.

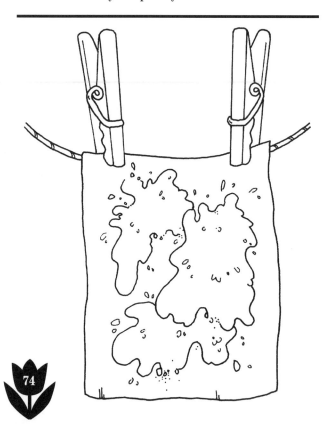

SIMPLE SUPPLIES

You'll need food coloring, water, scissors, plastic spray bottles, paint shirts, yarn, hinge-style clothespins, and 1×2-foot rectangles of cotton cloth such as old sheets or pillowcases. You'll also need a warm spring day.

DIRECTIONS

❶ Before class fill spray bottles with colored water. You'll need three spray bottles for every 10 children in your group. Outside, string yarn like a clothesline against a fence or between two trees. If your group is larger than 10, string a 12-foot section of yarn for every 10 children. Recruit an adult helper for each small group.

❷ Give each child a piece of cloth and two clothespins and help children attach the cloths to the clothesline one foot apart.

❸ Have children put on paint shirts or grocery sacks with arm and head holes cut out. Then have them stand 3-feet away from their cloths.

❹ Give the spray bottles to children and let them squirt their cloths then pass the spray bottles down the line. Point out how the colors mix to form new colors.

❺ Tell parents to toss the cloths in their dryers for five to 10 minutes to set the color. Children may use the cloths as flags, bandannas, or capes.

EXTRA FUN

When children are finished spraying their cloths, lead them in singing this fun song to the tune of "Row, Row, Row Your Boat." Let children wave their cloths like flags as they sing.

Spray, spray, spray the cloth.
Colors look so bright!
Pretty flags fly in the wind
Like rainbows in the sky!

Blooming Bonnets

SIMPLE SUPPLIES

You'll need sturdy paper plates, scissors, markers, glue sticks, and construction paper.

DIRECTIONS

❶ Before class cut the paper plates in half. Then cut out the arches, forming a C-shaped visor for each child.

❷ Set out construction paper, glue sticks, and markers. Give each child a paper visor, then have children color their visors. Then encourage children to tear colorful construction paper "petals" to glue on their visors.

❸ Show children how to slip the ends of the visors behind their ears to make fancy "bonnets" to wear.

EXTRA FUN

Form two groups, the Finders and the Flowers. Have the Flowers wear their visors. Tell children that the Finders want to pick the Flowers to make beautiful bouquets! On your signal, allow the Flowers to hop around the room while the Finders take giant steps. When a Finder tags a Flower, the Flower takes off his or her visor and helps "pick" flowers. When there is only one Flower left, have groups switch roles and play again.

CRAFTY TIPS

✔ Wallpaper samples make bright and decorative flower petals. These samples are free at many paint, decorating, or hardware stores. You'll need to use scissors to cut wallpaper petals.

✔ Sturdy plates with a flat (rather than bumpy) edge work best for this activity.

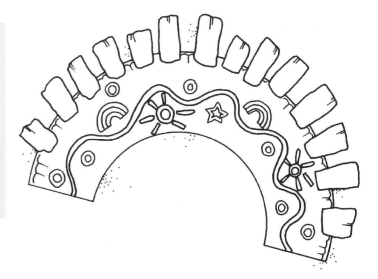

PART 4

Summer Spectaculars

Rainbow Hummers

✔ Use Rainbow Hummers in your lessons about Noah or about God's promises.

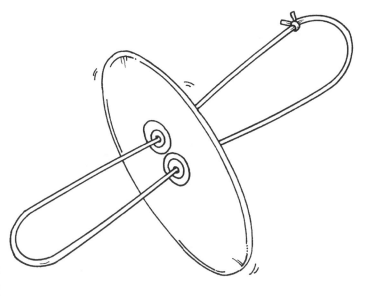

SIMPLE SUPPLIES

You'll need self-adhesive paper, scissors, a hole punch, plastic margarine-tub lids, and narrow 18-inch shoestrings or 18-inch lengths of string.

DIRECTIONS

❶ Before class cut the rims off the plastic margarine-tub lids. Make sure there are no jagged edges that could hurt little fingers.

❷ Cut self-adhesive paper into doughnut shapes small enough to fit two inside each lid. You'll need two doughnut shapes for each child.

❸ Use a hole punch to make two holes one-half-inch apart in the center of each lid. Make sure that the paper doughnuts do not cover the holes when placed on the lids.

❹ Set out the trimmed lids and the doughnut-shaped, self-adhesive paper. Have the children place the rings on the lids.

❺ Give each child each a shoestring or 18-inch length of string. Help him or her thread the shoestring through both holes, then tie the ends in a knot.

❻ Instruct children to move the plastic lids to the center of the shoestring loops. Show children how to hold the shoestring in both hands and twirl the hummer toward themselves to wind up the shoestring. After the children twirl their shoestrings, have children pull the ends away from each other, in a stretching motion, to make the hummers joyfully hum and spin.

EXTRA FUN

Let children spin their hummers while they say this action rhyme.

Spin, spin *(spin hummers)*,
Hummer sound—
Rainbow colors spinning 'round.
Spin me high. *(Hold hummers up.)*
Spin me low. *(Hold hummers down.)*
Spin me 'round *(turn around in place)*
Like a bright rainbow!

"The heavens tell the glory of God, and the skies announce what his hands have made" (Psalm 19:1).

Starry-Sky Paintings

TIPS   ✔ Use this idea with lessons on Creation or on God's promises to Abraham.

✔ You may want to tape the Starry-Sky Paintings to the ceiling of your classroom for a starry, starry Sunday school room.

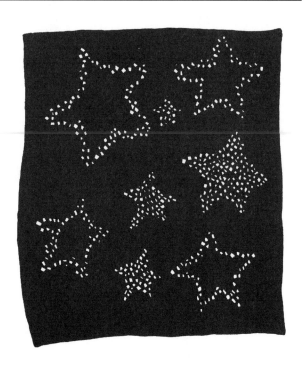

SIMPLE SUPPLIES

You'll need newspaper, white chalk, paintbrushes, salt, warm water, measuring cups and spoons, bowls, cookie sheets, and black or blue construction paper. You'll also need access to an oven.

DIRECTIONS

❶ Before class make enough saltwater to provide a half-filled bowl for every four children. To make saltwater, dissolve 3 teaspoons of salt in ¼ cup of warm water.

❷ Cover a table with newspaper. Set out bowls of saltwater. Give each child a sheet of construction paper, chalk, and a paintbrush.

❸ Have children draw star shapes with chalk on their papers.

❹ Invite children to dip their paintbrushes in saltwater then paint salty sparkles over the chalk star-shapes.

❺ Have a helper place the finished paintings on a cookie sheet and set them in an oven heated to 150 degrees for five minutes. When the water has dried, only the sparkling salt shapes will remain.

EXTRA FUN

Teach children this song to the tune of "Twinkle, Twinkle, Little Star" as the starry pictures dry. Then turn off the lights. Let children take turns shining a flashlight on their Starry-Sky Paintings.

Twinkle, twinkle, little star.
Oh, how beautiful you are.
God hung you up in the sky
To shine and twinkle way up high.
Twinkle, twinkle, little star.
Oh, how beautiful you are.

Puddles

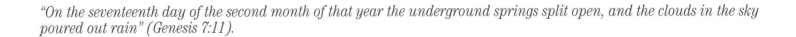

✔ Puddles are a nice addition to lessons about the 40 days and nights of rain during Noah's time.

✔ Clear packing tape may be used to reinforce the seams of the bags.

SIMPLE SUPPLIES

You'll need cornstarch, water, cooking oil, blue food coloring, clear packing tape, a measuring cup, and paper towels. You'll also need quart-size, heavy-duty, resealable freezer bags.

DIRECTIONS

1 Give each child a resealable freezer bag.

2 Help each child add ¼ cup of cornstarch to his or her bag. Add ¼ cup of water and two drops of blue food coloring to the cornstarch.

3 Remove the excess air from the bags, then seal them securely.

4 Invite children to gently squish the ingredients in their bags until the mixture is completely mixed, then have children bring the bags to you. Open each bag and add ¼ cup of cooking oil.

5 Again, remove the excess air from the bags, then seal them. Wipe the top edge of each bag with a paper towel so it's completely clean and dry. Show children how to fold over the top edges of the bags. Then help children seal the bags securely with clear packing tape.

6 Encourage the children to lay the bags flat on the table and press the ingredients gently with their fingers to see small puddles form and move from place to place. Invite children to let their fingers go for a "walk" across the puddles.

While the children are playing with their puddles, repeat the following rhyme.

EXTRA FUN

Puddles, puddles,
Here and there!
Puddles, puddles,
Everywhere!
Puddles, puddles,
Here and there,
Remind us God is everywhere.

Sand Castles

CRAFTY TIPS

✔ You may wish to have children wear paint shirts for this sand-sculpting activity.

✔ Provide a washtub of damp sand and let children make fingertip prints in the sand.

SIMPLE SUPPLIES

You'll need newspaper, scissors, pretzel sticks, tape, scraps of construction paper, a measuring cup, and fabric scraps. You'll also need a batch of sandy dough (the recipe is below).

DIRECTIONS

❶ Before class prepare a batch of special Sandy Dough. Its gritty texture will make the ocean seem close no matter where you're building your castle. You'll also need to prepare small fabric rectangles. Cut fabric in ½×¼-inch rectangles.

Sandy Dough
2 cups sand
4 cups flour
4 tablespoons alum
4 tablespoons baby oil

❷ Cover a table with newspaper. Give each child ½ cup of sandy dough. Encourage children to form beautiful sand castles.

❸ Give children scraps of colored paper and let them tear tiny, colorful bits to press into their completed castles.

❹ Set out pretzel sticks, tape, and fabric rectangles. Help children choose pieces of fabric and tape them to pretzel sticks to make flags for their castles.

EXTRA FUN

Create a clever castle kingdom on the table. Then let children march around the table and sing this joyful, jubilant song to the tune of "Here We Go 'Round the Mulberry Bush." Do the motions for extra fun.

Sandy castles on the beach *(hold arms in the air)*,
On the beach *(touch the floor)*,
On the beach. *(Touch the floor.)*
Sandy castles on the beach *(hold arms in the air)*
Standing in the sunshine.

Flags wave high up in the sky *(wave arms in the air)*,
In the sky *(jump up)*,
In the sky. *(Jump up.)*
Flags wave high up in the sky *(wave arms in the air)*
On our sandy castles.

Neckties for Daddy

✔ Try making bow ties for fancier fun.

SIMPLE SUPPLIES

You'll need colored construction paper, tape, scissors, star and heart stickers, and colorful markers.

DIRECTIONS

❶ Before class cut a construction paper necktie shape for each child.

❷ Set out star stickers, heart stickers, and markers. Give each child a tie shape. Invite children to decorate the ties using stickers and markers. Ask children why their dads are all-star daddies. Write a few of their comments on the back of the ties as children are working.

❸ Tape the neckties to children's shirts. Tell them to be sure to give the ties to their daddies, grandpas, or other caregivers.

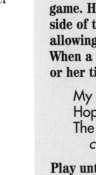

EXTRA FUN

Let children wear their decorated ties while they play this active game. Have children stand on one side of the room. Repeat the rhyme, allowing children to take turns calling out colors. When a color is named, each child with that color on his or her tie may hop to the other side of the room.

> My necktie is pretty and bright.
> Hop across the room if the color is right.
> The color is (name a color). *(Point to a different child each time to call out the color).*

Play until each child has called out a color. Vary the game by asking children to tiptoe or crawl across the room.

My Daddy plays checkers with me.

Eagles' Wings

CRAFTY TIPS

✔ Use this craft idea when teaching about how the birds brought food to Elijah.

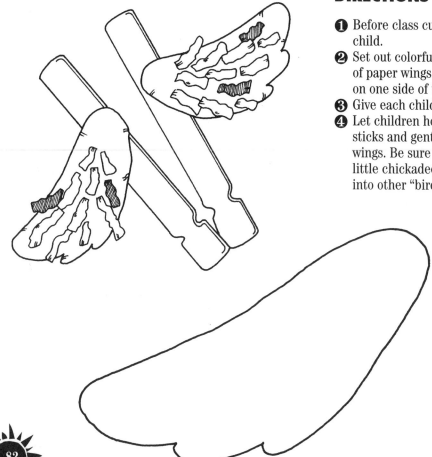

SIMPLE SUPPLIES

You'll need paper grocery sacks, construction paper, scissors, glue sticks, and tape. You'll also need two paint sticks for each child. Paint sticks are free from most paint or hardware stores.

DIRECTIONS

❶ Before class cut grocery sacks into large wing shapes. You'll need a pair of paper wings for each child.

❷ Set out colorful sheets of construction paper, paint sticks, and glue sticks. Give each child a pair of paper wings. Invite children to tear feather shapes from the construction paper and glue them on one side of their wings.

❸ Give each child two paint sticks. Help children tape the paint sticks to the back of the wings.

❹ Let children hold the paint sticks and gently flap their new wings. Be sure to remind your little chickadees not to bump into other "birds."

Let children stretch their wings as they "fly" with this action rhyme.

EXTRA FUN

> Fly like an eagle way up high.
> Stretch your wings and reach for the sky.
> Fly to the left;
> Fly to the right.
> Fly all day;
> Fly all night.
> Fly up high;
> Swoop down low.
> Fly like an eagle
> Wherever you go.

Sand Paintings

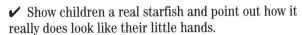

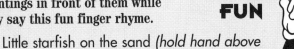

SIMPLE SUPPLIES

You'll need crayons, star stickers, plastic spoons, construction paper, craft glue, cotton swabs, pie pans, and dry sand.

DIRECTIONS

❶ Set out crayons. Give each child a sheet of construction paper and have children draw ocean waves on the bottom of their papers. Encourage children to color the waves with watery colors like blues and greens.

❷ When children have finished coloring, set out pie pans containing craft glue. Give each child a cotton swab to dab glue above the waves on the picture.

❸ Place pie pans containing sand and plastic spoons on the table. Let children sprinkle spoonfuls of sand over the glue on their pictures. Shake the excess sand back into the pie pans.

❹ Give children extra sheets of construction paper and let them tear small seashell shapes to add to the sandy part of their pictures.

❺ Hand each child a star-sticker "starfish" to add to the beach.

> **EXTRA FUN**
>
> Let children place their Sand Paintings in front of them while they say this fun finger rhyme.
>
> Little starfish on the sand *(hold hand above picture),*
> You look just like my little hand. *(Wiggle fingers on hand.)*

CRAFTY TIPS

✔ Have a variety of larger seashells hidden around the room for the children to find.

✔ Show children a real starfish and point out how it really does look like their little hands.

Red, White, and Berry Blue

CRAFTY TIPS

✔ Invite parents or other caregivers to a "Berry Blue, We Love You!" Party. Serve these special treats and let children share things they're thankful for.

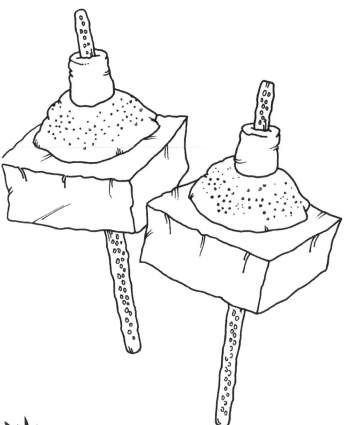

SIMPLE SUPPLIES

You'll need blue or purple finger gelatin, strawberries, mini-marshmallows, plastic knives, paper plates, plastic bowl, pretzel sticks, and paint shirts.

DIRECTIONS

❶ Before this activity make a pan of blue finger gelatin and cut it into squares.

❷ Have children wash their hands and put on paint shirts or grocery sacks with holes cut out for arms and heads. Then invite children to form groups of three.

❸ Give each group three plastic knives, an empty bowl, and a small bowl of strawberries.

❹ Show children how to cut the berries in half, take the stems off, and drop the berries in the empty bowl.

❺ When children have cut all their berries, have each group form an assembly line. Give each group six mini-marshmallows, three empty paper plates, a plate with six gelatin cubes on it, and pretzel sticks. Each group will need six pretzel sticks and a few extras to munch on.

❻ Instruct the first child in each group to place a square of blue finger gelatin on a plate, the second to put half a berry on the gelatin, then the last child to place a mini-marshmallow on the top and poke a pretzel stick through the whole thing. Continue until there are two treats for each child.

EXTRA FUN

As children build each layer of their red, white, and blue snacks, have them tell their groups things they're thankful for. Before everyone enjoys the snacks together, have a few volunteers share what they talked about. Then pray and thank God for all the good things he's given us.

Sandy Seashores

SIMPLE SUPPLIES

You'll need a small plastic bottle or jar with a lid for each child, water, blue food coloring, sand, mineral oil, cotton swabs, glue, and a plastic funnel.

DIRECTIONS

❶ Before class collect plastic bottles or jars for children. Be sure the bottles and jars have tight-fitting lids. (Sample-size baby-oil bottles would be ideal because they provide both the bottles and the mineral oil that you'll need for this activity.)

❷ Give each child a plastic bottle or jar half-filled with water. Add a few drops of food coloring.

❸ Use a funnel and let children help put sand in their containers. The sand should fill the bottom one-fourth of each container.

❹ Set out glue and cotton swabs. Give children the lids to their containers. Have children use the cotton swabs to put glue all around the inside rim of the lids.

❺ Leaving the containers on the table, use the funnel to add mineral or baby oil to fill each Sandy Seashore. Leave as little air space as possible. Help children screw on the gluey lids to seal their Sandy Seashores.

❻ Show children how to hold the bottles sideways and tilt their Sandy Seashores to create waves.

CRAFTY TIPS

✔ Make this craft sparkle by adding glitter to the sand before putting it in the water.

✔ Use this craft when you tell stories about storms. Let the children shake the bottles hard to create storms.

EXTRA FUN

Let the children tip their bottles from side to side as you reinforce the Creation story with this short poem which you can also sing together to the tune of "The Farmer in the Dell."

God spoke and made an ocean.
God spoke and made a sea.
God spoke and made the wind and waves,
A gift for you and me!

Chalky Fireworks

✔ Use this colorful craft to celebrate the New Year.

SIMPLE SUPPLIES

You'll need colored chalk, measuring cups, measuring spoons, water, sugar, cups or bowls, a spoon, napkins, and black construction paper.

DIRECTIONS

❶ Before class mix sugar and water in the following proportions: ½ cup of water to 2 tablespoons of sugar. Stir until dissolved. Make 1 cup for every 10 pieces of chalk.

❷ Place sticks of colored chalk in the sugar-water and let them soak for five minutes.

❸ Set out pieces of presoaked chalk on napkins. Give each child a piece of black construction paper and invite children to make fireworks designs on their papers, using different colors of chalk.

❹ Encourage children to make different strokes, squiggles, dots, waves, and lines in random patterns. The treated chalk will be brighter and leave fewer smudges than plain chalk.

EXTRA FUN

Move the chalky fireworks outdoors. Give each child a piece of chalk and tell children that they will get to pretend to be firecrackers. Have them scatter around on the playground pavement, sidewalk, or parking lot. When you say, "Firecrackers, POP," have them draw chalky fireworks designs on the pavement. When you call out, "Jesus sets you free," have them stop drawing and act like firecrackers. Encourage children to jump up and down, wave their arms, move around, and make firecracker noises such as "pop," "bang," and "boom!"

Green-Pastures Snacks

SIMPLE SUPPLIES

You'll need paper plates, a plastic knife, plastic spoons, a plastic quart jar with a tight-fitting lid, instant pistachio pudding mix, milk, blueberry gelatin, red licorice ropes, and small cookies with jelly centers.

DIRECTIONS

❶ Before class prepare blueberry gelatin according to the instructions on the package. Cut the gelatin into ½-inch chunks.

❷ Form three groups: the Shakers, the Givers, and the Cutters. Have an adult helper work with each of the three groups.

❸ Pour milk into the quart jar. Add the pistachio pudding mix and have the Shakers take turns shaking it until the pudding has thickened.

❹ Have the Givers put a paper plate, a spoon, and two or three cookies at each child's place.

❺ Have the Cutters break the licorice ropes into pieces the same width as the paper plates and distribute two pieces to each child.

❻ When the groups have finished their work, gather everyone around a table. Demonstrate how to lay the licorice ropes across the center of a plate about two inches apart to "draw" a stream.

❼ Drop blue gelatin cubes into each child's stream and have the children use plastic spoons to smear the gelatin to fill the streams.

❽ Put a dollop of pistachio pudding above the stream and a dollop below.

❾ After children have smeared the pudding to fill the plates on either side of the stream, show them how to add cookie "flowers" beside the stream.

❿ Invite children to gobble up their landscapes.

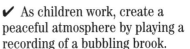

✔ As children work, create a peaceful atmosphere by playing a recording of a bubbling brook.

✔ Use this crafty snack during a lesson on how God takes care of us and provides everything we need.

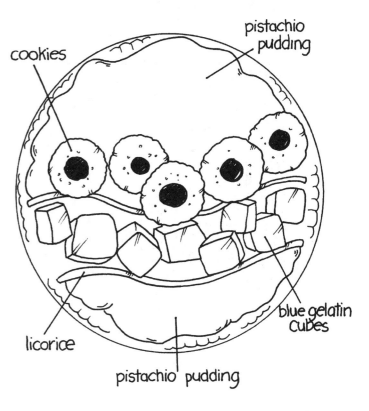

cookies

pistachio pudding

licorice

blue gelatin cubes

pistachio pudding

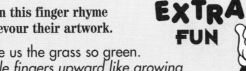

Teach children this finger rhyme before they devour their artwork.

God gave us the grass so green. *(Wiggle fingers upward like growing grass.)*
God gave us the bubbling stream. *(Wiggle fingers back and forth.)*
God made the flowers all pretty and bright. *(Fan hands around your face.)*
God takes care of us day and night. *(Hug yourself.)*

Summer Stars

CRAFTY TIPS

✔ You can use metallic confetti designed for different holidays. Other bits and pieces are fun to insert as well. Look at how they respond to the pull of the static electricity.

✔ As always when using balloons, do this project under strict adult supervision and make sure children do not put balloons near their mouths.

✔ Tie colorful ribbons and stars around the knots of the balloons for tails.

SIMPLE SUPPLIES

You'll need 11-inch clear or white balloons; red and blue metallic star garland; scissors; and empty, dry, plastic soda bottles.

DIRECTIONS

❶ Before class strip the stars off the garland using the scissors' blade.

❷ Set out soda bottles and metallic stars. Have the children place the stars in the bottles.

❸ When children have as many stars as they want in the bottles, help them stretch the necks of the balloons over the necks of the bottles.

❹ Have children turn the bottles upside down and shake the stars into the balloons.

❺ Blow up the balloons for the children. Have extra adult helpers available to assist children. Be careful to remove the balloon from your mouth when you inhale so that you don't suck in a star! Tie off each balloon.

❻ Instruct children to rub the balloons on their hair. Then watch the stars jump around and cling to the sides of the balloons in different patterns.

EXTRA FUN

Cut a construction paper star for each child and tape the stars to the floor. Have each child stand on a star, holding a summer-star balloon. Say, "Twinkle, stars," and have children bop their balloons to another star. End by singing "Twinkle, Twinkle, Little Star" as children bop their balloons up and down.

Crumpled Fish

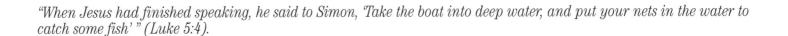

SIMPLE SUPPLIES

You'll need clear fold-top sandwich bags, several colors of tissue paper, transparent tape, and a black permanent marker.

DIRECTIONS

❶ Set out tissue paper. Give each child a clear sandwich bag.

❷ Have children tear tissue paper into small pieces. Invite them to crumple the pieces of tissue loosely and to fill their clear sandwich bags with the pieces.

❸ Tape the open end of the bags closed.

❹ Help children use the black permanent marker to add eyes, fins, and smiles.

EXTRA FUN

Have children play Fisherman's Net. Lay a blanket on the floor in the middle of the classroom. Have children place all of the fish in the middle of the blanket, then have children hold on to the edge of the blanket and lift it waist-high with the fish still in the middle. Encourage children to begin raising and lowering the blanket quickly, making the fish jump. Have the children work together to flip the fish off the blanket. The fish will flip and flop right out of the "net." Giggles and laughter are a guaranteed "catch of the day" when you play this fishy game.

CRAFTY TIPS

✔ Crumpled Fish are a delightful addition to lessons about the loaves and fish, fishers of people, God's creation of all sea life, or Jonah and the fish.

✔ Let children make several fish to tape onto a deep-sea bulletin board for your classroom.

Seashore Starfish

CRAFTY TIPS

✔ Make an ocean scene on a piece of poster board. Glue on cornmeal "sand" and add other items such as shells, rocks, and seaweed.

✔ Add some other ocean items such as coral, seashells, or kelp to help children envision the wonderful world below the sea.

SIMPLE SUPPLIES

You'll need cornmeal; glue; water; cotton swabs; pie pans; large box lids or flat boxes; a star stencil; a pencil; scissors; and poster board in orange, blue, and fluorescent colors.

DIRECTIONS

❶ Before class cut starfish from poster board. Provide one fish in each color for each child. Dilute one part of water to two parts of glue.

❷ Set out starfish shapes, cotton swabs, and pie pans half-full of diluted glue. Let children dab glue on one side of the starfish shapes.

❸ Have children place their sticky starfish shapes sticky-side-up in the large box lids or flat boxes. Sprinkle cornmeal on their starfish shapes and shake off the excess. Use the cornmeal left in the boxes as you continue to coat the starfish.

❹ Let children make several different colors of starfish. Set them aside to dry for 10 minutes.

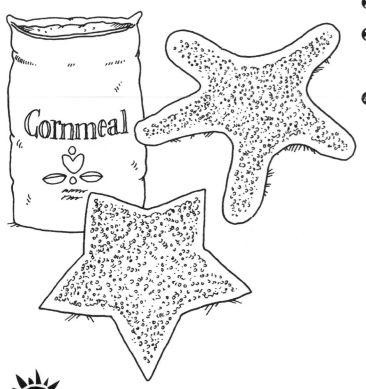

When the starfish are dry, let children hold their creatures and say this rhyme.

EXTRA FUN

Seashore Starfish glow upon the sand.
Seashore Starfish wiggle in my hand.
Seashore Starfish crawl upon the rocks.
Seashore Starfish creep upon my socks.

Rainbow Swirls

SIMPLE SUPPLIES

You'll need paper plates; newspaper; white crayons; spray bottles; water; large paintbrushes; paint shirts; pie pans; and thinned red, yellow, and blue tempera paint.

DIRECTIONS

❶ Before class cover your work area with newspaper.

❷ Give each child a paper plate.

❸ Help children use white crayons to write their first names across the middle of their plates. Go over the names three or four times so there's a heavy coating of crayon on the plates.

❹ Have children put on paint shirts or grocery sacks with holes cut out for arms and heads. Let children use spray bottles to moisten the middle of their plates. The plates should be moist but without puddles of water.

❺ Set out pie pans of thinned tempera paints in primary colors.

❻ Hand out paintbrushes and let children swish colors onto their moist plates then tip the plates so the colors run together. As the primary colors blend, they'll form rainbows of colors with the children's names shining through.

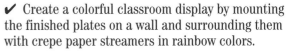

CRAFTY TIPS

✔ Children may wish to make rainbow nameplates for other members of their families.

✔ Create a colorful classroom display by mounting the finished plates on a wall and surrounding them with crepe paper streamers in rainbow colors.

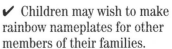 **EXTRA FUN**

Use the finished plates in a fun affirmation time. Gather everyone in a circle. Teach children this cheer, then have children repeat it for each child. Have children take turns standing in the center of the circle.

(Name of child), (name of child), we're glad
   you're you!
We love you and God does too!

Sailboat Snacks

✔ Invite parents and care-givers to visit. Have children make Sailboat Snacks for their guests.

✔ This is a great snack idea to use with the stories of Jonah and Noah.

SIMPLE SUPPLIES

You will need sturdy paper plates, a rolling pin, pretzel sticks, leaf lettuce, a bowl, peaches, a knife, and sliced sandwich bread.

DIRECTIONS

❶ Before class remove crusts from bread slices and cut each slice into two triangles. You'll need one triangle for each child. Cut peaches in half and remove the pits.

❷ Set out lettuce in a bowl. Give each child a paper plate and three lettuce leaves. Let children cover their plates with three lettuce leaves.

❸ Place a half-peach "boat" on each child's plate of lettuce.

❹ Set out the bread triangles and the rolling pin. Let children take turns rolling their bread triangles into flat sails for their boats.

❺ Give children pretzel sticks for masts. Show children how to thread the pretzel sticks through the flattened bread slices then push the pretzel sticks into the ships for sails.

EXTRA FUN

Before the children devour their fruity snacks, have them sail their boats to this little rhyme.

Sailing, sailing through stormy
    seas—
Jesus is always here with me!
I'm safe in my little sailboat;
With Jesus I'll always stay afloat.
I'm happy sailing with him every day.
He loves me and by my side he will stay.

"Cows and bears will eat together in peace. Their young will lie down to rest together. Lions will eat hay as oxen do" *(Isaiah 11:7).*

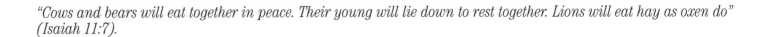

Cinnamon Teddy Bear Biscuits

SIMPLE SUPPLIES

You'll need a cookie sheet, aluminum foil, a small dish of melted butter, a pastry brush, a shaker jar of cinnamon-sugar, wet wipes, and three refrigerator biscuits for each child. You'll also need access to an oven.

DIRECTIONS

1 Give each child a small square of aluminum foil and three refrigerator biscuits.
2 Demonstrate how to make a biscuit bear by using two whole biscuits for the head and body and pinching off dough from the third biscuit to add ears, arms, and legs.
3 Help children brush melted butter on their bears, then sprinkle them with cinnamon-sugar.
4 Have an adult helper transfer the aluminum-foil square to a cookie sheet and bake the bears according to the biscuit-package directions.
5 Clean up sticky fingers with wet wipes.

EXTRA FUN

When the baked bears have cooled slightly, let children take them to a teddy bears' picnic. Spread an old blanket or plastic table cloth on a grassy spot outdoors or on the floor indoors if the weather doesn't cooperate. Let children march to the picnic area singing a lively chorus of "This Is the Day" or "If You're Happy and You Know It."

CRAFTY TIPS

✔ Have each preschooler make two bears, then let children serve their extra bears on colorful napkins to children from another class during a lesson on sharing.

Summer Shivers

CRAFTY TIPS

✔ Mix leftover condiments with the chocolate or the honey and drop teaspoons onto a greased cookie sheet. Freeze this mixture for some yummy candy treats to share with another class.

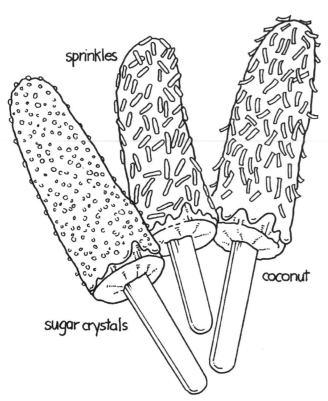

sprinkles

coconut

sugar crystals

SIMPLE SUPPLIES

You will need bananas; a knife; craft sticks; paper plates; pie pans; napkins; damp washcloths; and toppings such as honey, finely chopped nuts, cake decorating sprinkles, cookie crumbs, melted chocolate, and coconut. You will also need access to a freezer.

DIRECTIONS

❶ Before class peel bananas and cut them in half widthwise. Push a craft stick up the center of each half, then place bananas in the freezer overnight.

❷ Put toppings in separate pie pans and set them out on the table. Give each child a frozen banana on a stick and a paper plate.

❸ Let children create their own taste sensations by rolling the frozen bananas in honey or melted chocolate and then dipping them in any or all of the other condiments.

❹ Have children put their bananas on their plates. Make sure each child has a napkin.

❺ Clean up sticky fingers and faces with damp washcloths.

EXTRA FUN

After children eat their Summer Shivers, let children join in an active rhyme.

Summer time is oh, so fun *(exaggerated smile)—*
Time to laugh and time to run. *(Run in place.)*
How I love the summer sun *(make big circle with your arms)*
That God lets shine for everyone. *(Sweep arms out at sides.)*

Bubble-Print Place Mats

SIMPLE SUPPLIES

You will need plain white paper, bubble solution, four plastic dishpans, water, a measuring cup, drinking straws, food coloring, a black marker, and newspaper.

DIRECTIONS

❶ Before children arrive pour bubble solution into four dishpans. You'll need an inch of bubble solution in each dishpan. Add a cup of water and five drops of food coloring to each pan. Use a set of food coloring to provide blue, red, green, and yellow. You'll also need to cut an 8×11-inch white paper "place mat" for each child.

❷ Cover your work area with newspaper.

❸ Set out dishpans of bubble solution. Give each child a drinking straw and a place mat. Have children practice blowing through their straws while you write their names on the back of the place mats with the black marker.

❹ Allow each child to take a turn placing one end of the straw in the bubble solution and blowing into the other end to make a dishpan full of colored bubbles.

❺ Let children gently hold their place mats on top of the bubbles for a few seconds.

❻ Help children carefully remove their place mats from the bubbles to reveal beautiful, bubbly designs.

❼ Allow children to repeat the process, using the different-colored solutions you've set out.

EXTRA FUN

While children are waiting for their place mats to dry, take a few containers of bubble solution and bubble wands outside. Have children take turns blowing and "catching" bubbles while you lead them in this song to the tune of "Are You Sleeping?"

Blowing bubbles *(point to bubbles in air),*
Blowing bubbles *(point to bubbles in air),*
With my friends *(give a high five or hug),*
With my friends. *(Give a high five or hug.)*
Bubbles are such fun. *(Clap on each word.)*
Jump high and you'll catch one. *(Jump up and try to catch a bubble.)*
Pop, pop, pop. *(Flick fingers like popping bubbles.)*
Pop, pop, pop. *(Flick fingers like popping bubbles.)*

Allow each child to have a turn blowing bubbles for the song.

CRAFTY TIPS

✔ It's best to use a premade bubble solution since these usually don't irritate children's eyes or skin.

✔ Try this art activity outside and have children set their place mats on the ground. Let them use a bubble wand to blow bubbles that will land and pop on their place mats.

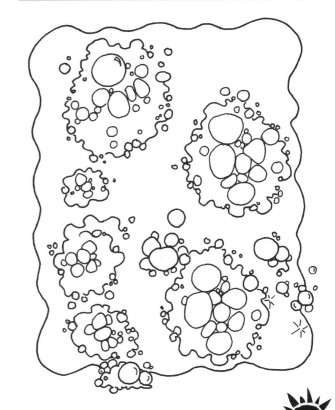

Fly-Swatter Paintings

CRAFTY TIPS

✔ Let children glue bits of colored, paper confetti to their pictures as summertime bugs.

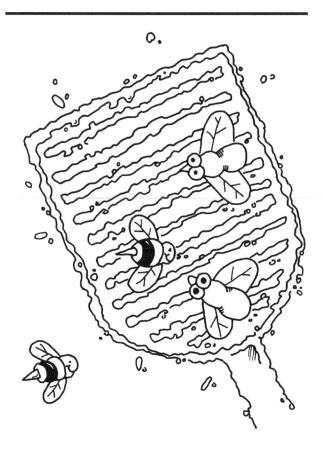

SIMPLE SUPPLIES

You'll need paint shirts, black markers, paper, tempera paint, cake pans, and old fly-swatters.

DIRECTIONS

❶ This project is best done outside. Have children put on paint shirts or paper grocery sacks with holes cut out for heads and arms.

❷ On the grass, set out shallow cake pans of tempera paint and fly-swatters for each paint pan. Hand children paper and markers and invite them to draw some pesky summertime bugs such as flies, mosquitoes, and gnats.

❸ Have children spread out around the grass, then let them take turns gently "swatting" the bugs on their papers with fly-swatters lightly dipped in paint. Encourage them to use different colors for interesting effects.

EXTRA FUN

When the pictures are dry, let children play a fun game with raisin "bugs." Have children line their pictures up on the ground or floor then stand three feet away from the pictures. Hand each child five raisins. Have the children try to toss the raisin bugs onto the pictures between the fly-swatter prints. After all the bugs have been tossed, collect them and play again. After the game, throw out the used raisins and hand children fresh raisins to enjoy.

Hoppity Frogs

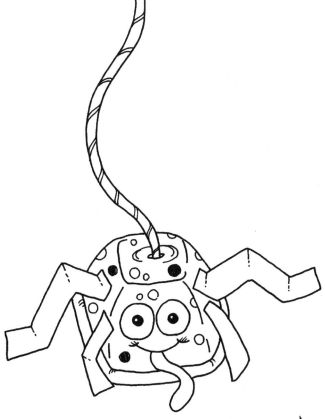

SIMPLE SUPPLIES

You'll need egg cartons, construction paper scraps, glue, tape, ¼-inch dot stickers, scissors, crayons or markers, and string.

DIRECTIONS

1 Before class cut egg cartons into 12 individual cups. Poke a small hole in the bottom of each cup. Cut string into 12-inch lengths. Knot one end of each string and thread a length of string up through the bottom of each cup.

2 Give each child an egg-carton cup with string. Set out glue, tape, construction paper scraps, and crayons or markers. Let the children tear construction paper scraps to form legs.

3 Set out the dot stickers and have children put stickers in place for eyes.

4 Let children add other special touches to their frogs, such as tongues or polka dots.

> **EXTRA FUN**
>
> Read stories about frogs and toads, such as *Frog & Toad Are Friends* by Arnold Lobel, and let the children hop along with the stories. Also, say this catchy rhyme as the children frolic with their frog friends.
>
> Ribbit, ribbit,
> Hop, hop, hop.
> Ribbit, ribbit,
> Kersplash, plop!

CRAFTY TIPS

✔ Make other hopping creatures like rabbits or spiders and let children tell a story—using their creatures—about life on the ark.

Kaleidoscope Color-Tubes

CRAFTY TIPS

✔ If you can't locate enough cardboard bathroom-tissue tubes, make them from construction paper.

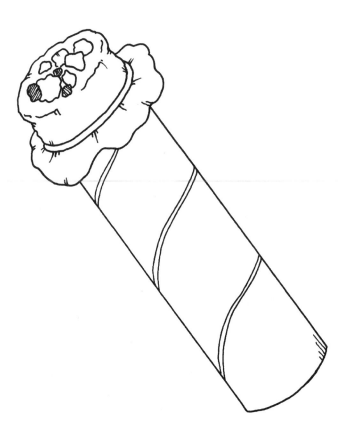

SIMPLE SUPPLIES

You'll need cardboard bathroom-tissue tubes, wax paper, colored tissue paper, glue, water, pie pans, cotton swabs, and rubber bands.

DIRECTIONS

❶ Before class dilute glue with an equal amount of water and place the diluted glue in pie pans.

❷ Give each child a bathroom-tissue tube, a 3-inch square of wax paper, and a rubber band.

❸ Set out the colored tissue paper, cotton swabs, and pie pans of diluted glue. Show children how to tear small pieces of tissue then use cotton swabs and glue to stick them to the wax paper.

❹ Have children continue until their wax paper squares are full of colored tissue.

❺ Place the wax paper squares in a sunny place to dry for 15 minutes. While the glue and tissue are drying, have children play the game in the Extra Fun section.

❻ Then help children place the wax paper over one end of their bathroom-tissue tubes, fastening them with rubber bands.

❼ Show children how to look at a window through the open end of their kaleidoscopes to see the bright colors.

EXTRA FUN

While the glue and tissue paper dry, take children outside with their cardboard tubes. Have children look through their tubes and say the following rhyme.

Looking up *(look up)*
And looking down *(look down),*
What do you see when you look around?
(Look around, then freeze on the word "around.")

Call on a few children to tell you what they see through their tubes. Children may see things such as a friend's ear, a tree, a bird, or a hot sidewalk. After two or three children have shared, lead children in prayer, thanking God for the things they've seen. Repeat the game until each child has had a turn to share.

PART 5

Holiday Happenings

Handy Paper Angels

CRAFTY TIPS

✔ Let children "fly" their angels around the room as you play a favorite Christmas song.

✔ Use this angelic craft during lessons on Jacob, Abraham and Sarah, or Peter in prison.

SIMPLE SUPPLIES

You'll need dark blue construction paper, white construction paper, scissors, glue, cotton swabs, a pie pan, pencils, large white paper doilies, facial tissues, and narrow white ribbon.

DIRECTIONS

❶ Before class cut sheets of blue and white construction paper so you have two 6×9-inch pieces for each child. Then fold the pieces in half to make 6×4½-inch cards. Cut narrow white ribbon into 6-inch lengths, providing one piece for each child.

❷ Give each child one pre-cut sheet of both blue and white construction paper and a pencil. Help each preschooler lay one hand on the white paper with the thumb laying along the fold. Then have adult helpers assist children in tracing their hands. Have adults cut out the hand tracings, taking care not to cut the fold of the papers.

❸ Invite children to open the hand shapes to form "wings." Set out glue in a pie pan and give each child a cotton swab. Help preschoolers glue the wings inside the folded blue cards so the tips of the fingers touch the tops of the blue cards.

❹ Give each child a large paper doily, two facial tissues, and a 6-inch length of narrow white ribbon. Show children how to wad the facial tissues into a ball, press the ball into the center of the doily, and pinch the doily together under the ball to form a head. Have adult helpers tie a white ribbon around the "neck" of each doily.

❺ Help each child put two lines of glue near the center of the wings and press the doily against the glue. The bottom of the angel should be even with the bottom of the card. When the glue dries, the angel will stand on its own. Allow 15 minutes of drying time for Handy Paper Angels.

EXTRA FUN

Explain to children that when Jesus was born, an angel appeared to shepherds and told the shepherds that the Christ child had been born in Bethlehem. Then have the children form two lines that face each other. Teach the first two lines of the following rhyme to one group and the second two lines to the other group. Let the children wave their angels as they say the rhyme to each other.

Angels white, angels bright,
Angels in the sky tonight.
"Go to Bethlehem," they say.
"See the baby in the hay."

Sculpted Trees

SIMPLE SUPPLIES

You'll need green poster board, tacky craft glue, pie pans, cotton swabs, tape, green food coloring, star stickers, flaked coconut, a plastic bowl, and colored construction paper.

DIRECTIONS

❶ Before class make cone-shaped "trees" from 8-inch green poster-board circles. Tape the edges of the cones securely. Prepare green coconut by stirring a few drops of green food coloring in a bowl of flaked coconut.

❷ Set out green coconut, cotton swabs, construction paper, and pie pans filled with glue. Give each child a cone-shaped tree. Invite children to use cotton swabs to spread glue on their trees then roll the trees in flaked coconut or sprinkle the coconut on to create pine needles.

❸ Let children tear small construction paper shapes and glue the "ornaments" on their trees. Add sticky stars to the treetops. Allow the trees to dry for at least 10 minutes.

EXTRA FUN

Tell children that Christmas trees look bright and cheery and remind us of the joy we feel over Jesus' birthday. Have children parade around the classroom as they hold their trees and sing this song to the tune of "O Tannenbaum."

O Christmas tree, O Christmas tree,
We sing with joy to Jesus.
O Christmas tree, O Christmas tree,
We sing with joy to Jesus.
Your sparkly lights and star above
Remind us of our Savior's love.
O Christmas tree, O Christmas tree,
We sing with joy to Jesus.

CRAFTY TIPS

✔ To create a sparkling effect, add glitter to the craft glue. Small bits of aluminum foil or garland make striking sparklers.

✔ Make extra trees to use as party favors or centerpieces at church Christmas festivities and bazaars.

Edible Shepherd Staffs

CRAFTY TIPS

✔ Have children make a plateful of shepherd-staff cookies to share with a neighbor of the church or the people in a nursing home.

Peppermint Stick Cookies

⅓ cup crushed peppermints
⅓ cup sugar
½ cup shortening
½ cup butter
1 cup powdered sugar
1 egg
1 teaspoon vanilla extract
2½ cups all-purpose flour
1 teaspoon salt
red food coloring

Mix the candy and ⅓ cup of sugar in a bowl.

Cream the shortening and butter. Gradually add the powdered sugar. Add the egg and beat well. Mix in the remaining ingredients.

Tint half of the dough with red food coloring.

SIMPLE SUPPLIES

You'll need a batch of Peppermint Stick Cookie dough (recipe below), extra flour, cookie sheets, and measuring spoons. You'll also need access to an oven.

DIRECTIONS

❶ Before class prepare the cookie recipe.
❷ Sprinkle a bit of flour at each child's work space.
❸ Give each child 1 tablespoon of red dough and 1 tablespoon of white dough. Roll the dough into two ropes, then join the ropes by pinching them together at one end and twisting them in candy-cane fashion. Point out how the twisted ropes look like shepherds' staffs.
❹ Place the edible staffs on ungreased cookie sheets. Bake at 375 degrees for 9 minutes or until the edges begin to brown. Remove the cookies from the cookie sheets while they're warm, then immediately coat them with the peppermint-candy mixture. Cool completely, then eat and enjoy! (This recipe yields about 4 dozen cookies.)

EXTRA FUN

While the cookie staffs cool, explain that shepherds used staffs to keep their sheep with the flock. Point out that the shepherds who visited baby Jesus probably used staffs. When the cookies are cool, have children hold the cookies like shepherd staffs for this action rhyme.

I'm a little shepherd *(hold your staff in front of you)*
Walking on my way *(walk around the room)*;
Uphill *(walk on your tiptoes)*,
Downhill *(walk low on your heels)*,
To visit Jesus today! *(Hold your staff in the air.)*

Christmas Birthday Banners

SIMPLE SUPPLIES

You'll need construction paper, scissors, stickers, crayons, colored chalk, markers, glue sticks, tape, and drinking straws.

DIRECTIONS

❶ Before class cut construction paper into triangular pennant shapes or long rectangles. You'll need one "banner" for each child.

❷ Set out construction paper, glue sticks, crayons, colored chalk, markers, and stickers. Give each child a paper banner, then invite children to decorate their banners using the craft materials. Encourage children to decorate both sides of their banners.

❸ When children have finished decorating their banners, help them tape drinking straws on as flagpoles.

CRAFTY TIPS

✔ At the beginning of the year, let each child make a birthday banner. As each child celebrates his or her birthday, let banners "fly" and let the birthday child take his or her special banner home.

EXTRA FUN

Tell children that banners are flags we wave to celebrate special events. Remind children that birthdays are special events and the most special birthday of all is Christmas—Jesus' birthday. Let children sing "Happy Birthday" to Jesus as they march around the room and wave their celebratory banners high in the sky!

Happy birthday to you.
Happy birthday to you.
Happy birthday, dear Jesus!
Oh, yes, we love you!

103

Three Kings

CRAFTY TIPS

✔ Don't hesitate to use unusual colors for the wise men's beards, such as orange, purple, or turquoise.

✔ This craft easily adapts to stories of Old Testament kings.

SIMPLE SUPPLIES

You'll need markers, a pencil, glitter glue, tape, glue, plain paper cups, scissors, and construction paper.

DIRECTIONS

❶ Before class cut several crowns and beards from different colors of construction paper. Size them to fit the paper cups you'll be using. Curl the beards by rolling them around a pencil. Make interesting eyes by cutting out some small circles and some large circles from construction paper. Glue the small circles on top of the large circles to make "googly" eyes.
Make a sample wise man by turning a cup upside down and taping a crown around the top, a beard to the bottom, and eyes in between.

❷ Give each child three paper cups and six googly eyes. Help children write their initials inside their cups with permanent markers.

❸ Set out glitter glue, tape, crowns and beards. Encourage each child to choose three crowns and three beards. Have them decorate the crowns with markers or glitter glue then wrap the crowns around the tops of the cups and tape them in place. Have children glue the googly eyes in place then add curly beards with glue or tape.

EXTRA FUN

Talk about how far the wise men traveled and followed the star to find baby Jesus. Then play this fun traveling game.

Cut a star from bright yellow paper. Hand the star to a child. Have the rest of the children balance one wise man each on their heads then carry the other wise men on their hands with their palms out flat in front of them. Have the children walk carefully, balancing their wise men, as the Star leads them slowly around the room. After one turn around the room, let a different child be the Star.

Candy-Cane Holders

SIMPLE SUPPLIES

You'll need rubber bands, scissors, curling ribbon or foil garland, silk holly, and candy canes.

DIRECTIONS

❶ Before class cut curling ribbon or foil garland into 12-inch lengths. You'll need one 12-inch length for each child.

❷ Give each child three candy canes and a rubber band. Show children how to hold three candy canes together upside down, with the curves of the candy canes pointing away from the center.

❸ Help children wrap rubber bands around their candy canes to hold them together then push the rubber bands down near the curves.

❹ Set out 12-inch lengths of curling ribbon or foil garland. Help each child wrap a length of curling ribbon or shiny foil garland around the rubber band several times to secure the arrangement and hide the rubber band.

❺ If you have plenty of adult helpers, have the helpers tie on several strands of curling ribbon to hide the rubber band then use scissors to curl the ends of the ribbon.

❻ Give each child a sprig of silk holly and show them how to push the stems of the holly inside the ribbons or garlands.

EXTRA FUN

Tell children that an angel told Mary and Joseph to name the Christ child Jesus. Explain to children that God knows each of us by name, too. Then play this fun name game. Have children stand in a circle and teach them this simple rhyme.

> I'm so glad that Jesus came
> And that Jesus knows your name.

Stand in the center of the circle. Have children say the rhyme, then point to a child and have that child shout his or her name. Then that child comes to the center and you take his or her place in the circle. Have everyone repeat the rhyme again, then have the child in the center point to another child. Continue until everyone has stood in the center. Have the last child point to you.

CRAFTY TIPS

✔ The children can make place cards for special Christmas guests and push the place cards between the tops of the candy canes. Explain that place cards make guests feel especially welcome.

✔ The candy canes can also hold special Christmas cards.

Recycled Hearts

CRAFTY TIPS

✔ Recycled Hearts can be used with lessons relating to God's love or Christian love for others.

✔ If you need computer paper edge strips, place an appeal in your church bulletin or call an office in your area that uses computers. You'll rapidly accumulate "miles" of them!

✔ Thread colorful cereal loops on the chenille wires in place of the paper strips.

SIMPLE SUPPLIES

You'll need a variety of colored chenille wires and edge strips from computer paper.

DIRECTIONS

❶ Give each child one chenille wire and four to five edge strips from computer paper.

❷ Let children use the chenille wires as needles to "sew" in and out of every other hole in the computer paper edge strips. (Hint: Keep the wires straight and bend the paper strips.)

❸ Show children how to slide the paper strips toward the middle after completing each strip.

❹ After children have finished sewing, have them twist the ends of their chenille wires together. Help children shape the chenille wires into heart shapes then spread the paper strips evenly around the edges.

EXTRA FUN

Point out how much Jesus loves us and how we want Jesus to live in our hearts. Then play an active game of Kiss and Toss with your Recycled Hearts.

Tape two drinking straws to the floor in an upright position. Have children stand three feet from either of the straws. Encourage children to kiss their Recycled Hearts then toss the hearts over one of the straws. Let children try for a ringer then collect their hearts and line up to play again.

Heart-Scent Love

✔ This craft idea makes a lovely gift for mommies or daddies!

SIMPLE SUPPLIES

You'll need potpourri, pastel construction paper, ribbon, scraps of lace, dried flowers, potpourri or cinnamon oil or vanilla, tacky craft glue, scissors, and a hole punch.

DIRECTIONS

❶ Before class cut heart shapes from 9×9-inch squares of the pastel construction paper. Punch a hole at the top of each curve of the heart. Cut ribbon into 6-inch lengths, then tie a ribbon through the holes of each heart to make a hanger. You'll need to prepare one paper heart for each child.

❷ Set out tacky craft glue, potpourri, scraps of lace, and dried flowers. Give each child a paper heart. Invite the children to glue potpourri and other items on the hearts. Encourage children to decorate the hearts completely so they'll look and smell pretty.

❸ When the hearts are finished, dab a bit of potpourri oil, cinnamon oil, or vanilla on the dried flowers to add a sweet scent. Allow the hearts to dry for 15 minutes.

EXTRA FUN

Play this fun game of Musical Hearts. Tape extra paper heart shapes to the floor in a circle. Provide at least one heart for each child. Be sure one heart is a bright color such as red or blue. Play music and have the children march around from heart to heart. When the music stops, the person standing on the bright heart shares something special about someone he or she loves. Continue playing, allowing everyone a turn to share. If a person is repeated, they may share again or have you start the music again.

I Love My Family

CRAFTY TIPS

✔ Use Valentine stickers and rubber stamps for special decorative touches.

✔ Make "I love you!" cards for people in the church who may not have families. Remind children that everyone belongs to God's family.

SIMPLE SUPPLIES

You'll need markers, crayons, scissors, paper doilies, bits of lace, tacky craft glue, pie pans, and cotton swabs. You'll also need 9×12-inch construction paper in Valentine colors such as red, pink, and white.

DIRECTIONS

❶ Before class fold 9×12-inch sheets of construction paper in half, then cut out heart shapes. Cut one paper heart for each child.

❷ Set out markers and crayons and give each child a heart shape. Help children trace their hands in the center of the hearts.

❸ Invite children to draw faces on the fingers of the hands to represent members of their families or special friends.

❹ Set out paper doilies, glue in pie pans, scraps of lace, and cotton swabs. Let children add their own creative touches to the Valentine cards.

EXTRA FUN

Remind children that God gave us families and friends to love. Point out that it's nice to give Valentine's Day cards to say, "I love you."

Let children hold their special cards and point to the members of their families as you lead them in singing this song to the tune of "Are You Sleeping?"

Where's my family? Where's my family?
Here we are. Here we are.
God made my fam'ly,
And we love each other.
Thank you, God.
Thank you, God.

Bouquets of Hearts

SIMPLE SUPPLIES

You'll need a variety of red and pink paper, wrapping paper, heart-shaped paper doilies, tape, plastic drinking straws, scissors, glue, cotton swabs, a pie pan, Valentine stickers, and large paper cups.

DIRECTIONS

❶ Before class cut out an assortment of paper hearts. Use red and pink paper and wrapping paper. Cut heart shapes in different sizes varying from 2-inch widths to 5-inch widths. You'll need six large and six small heart shapes for each child.
Cut drinking straws in half, providing six half-straws for each child.

❷ Give each child six straws, a paper cup, and a cotton swab. Provide glue in a shallow pie pan.

❸ Set out assorted heart shapes and heart doilies for children to choose. Show children how to put a solid paper heart behind a heart-shaped doily. Encourage children to glue wrapping paper on a plain heart.

❹ Help each child tape one end of every heart to the tip of each straw. (The straws become stems for heart bouquets!)

❺ Let children make colorful "vases" for their bouquets by decorating their paper cups with paper scraps and stickers.

CRAFTY TIPS

✔ Older preschoolers may want to further embellish their hearts by using glitter glue, curling ribbon, and stickers.

✔ Go as a group to deliver your heart bouquets to people who are special to children in your class. Have the children say the rhyme together then deliver a group hug!

Teach children this simple rhyme and encourage them to say it when they deliver their heart bouquets.

EXTRA FUN

When our hearts are full of love,
We know it comes from God above,
And I (we) LOVE YOU!

"They should praise him with dancing. They should sing praises to him with tambourines and harps" (Psalm 149:3).

Hosanna Streamers

CRAFTY TIPS

✔ Help children make up a streamer routine to accompany a favorite praise song then perform it for their parents.

✔ Adults enjoy these streamers too. Have each child make an extra streamer or two to share with adults for a special praise time.

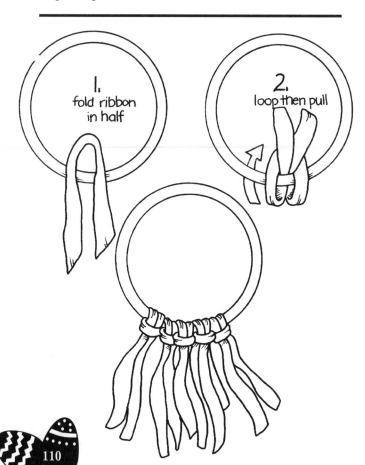

1. fold ribbon in half

2. loop then pull

SIMPLE SUPPLIES

You'll need plastic rings; scissors; and spools of curling ribbon in yellow, pink, blue, white, and light green.

DIRECTIONS

❶ Before class cut a 3-foot length of each color of ribbon for each child. Lay the ribbons in separate piles on a table.

❷ Have children name the colors as they take one ribbon from each pile.

❸ Give each child a plastic ring. (You may use the rings that hold soft drink cans together. Simply cut the rings apart to make six plastic rings. Or create plastic rings by cutting out the center of margarine-tub lids.)

❹ Show children how to fold a ribbon in half, put the folded edge through the ring, then pull the loose ends of the ribbon over the ring and through the folded end, pulling them tightly to create a knot around the ring. Older preschoolers will be able to do this in pairs. Younger preschoolers may need adult assistance. If an adult puts the folded end through the ring, a young preschooler can slip the loose ends through the folded end and tighten them.

❺ Help children put one of each color of ribbon on their plastic rings.

Teach children the following action rhyme and have them wave their streamers as they say it with you.

EXTRA FUN

Hosan-na! Hosan-na! *(Wave streamers overhead.)*
Here comes Jesus—can you see? *(Shield your eyes.)*
Hosan-na! Hosan-na! *(Wave streamers overhead.)*
Wave your streamers, one, two, three. *(Shake streamers in front of you.)*
Hosan-na! Hosan-na! *(Wave streamers overhead.)*
Jesus loves you! Jesus loves me! *(Throw streamers up and catch them.)*

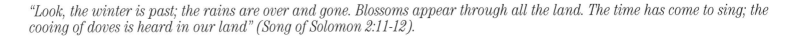

Growing Easter Baskets

SIMPLE SUPPLIES

You'll need potting soil, grass seeds, plastic spoons, newspaper, paint shirts, a permanent marker, a pitcher of water, pie pans, a spray bottle of water, and small containers such as margarine tubs or aluminum potpie pans.

DIRECTIONS

Plan to do this craft about two weeks before Easter. Let children know that it will take at least a week before they see little sprouts growing from their seeds.

1. Cover your work area with newspaper. Have children wear paint shirts or paper grocery sacks with holes cut out for arms and heads.
2. Set out margarine tubs or potpie pans, potting soil, and pie pans containing grass seeds.
3. Help each child choose a container and write his or her initials on the bottom with a permanent marker.
4. Give each child a plastic spoon. Show children how to carefully spoon potting soil into their containers until they're two-thirds full.
5. If the potting soil is dry, pour a little water in the containers and have children stir the water into the soil to dampen it.
6. Show children how to take a pinch of grass seeds and drop the seeds on the moistened soil.
7. After children have taken several pinches of seeds, show them how to lightly press the seeds into the dirt with their plastic spoons.
8. Help children spray just a bit of water on the seeds then carry their baskets to a sunny window. If the baskets are kept in a sunny, warm place, the grass seeds will begin to sprout in about a week. It's important to keep the soil slightly moist but not soggy.

Follow the planting activity with this action rhyme to help children understand what will happen to the seeds they planted.

EXTRA FUN

Down in the warm, soft dirt they go *(pretend to dig),*
Then God helps the tiny seeds to grow. *(Put hands together and move them slowly up.)*
Growing, growing, toward the light. *(Keep raising hands higher.)*
Tall grass, green grass, pretty and bright. *(Wave arms overhead.)*

CRAFTY TIPS

✔ You may want to keep the planted baskets in your classroom. You'll need to water them at least once during the week. If you choose to send the planted baskets home with the children, place them in plastic bags to prevent messy spills.

✔ On Easter Sunday let children place a few jelly bean "eggs" in their baskets. Talk about how eggs and new grass remind us of new life on the day we celebrate Jesus rising from the dead.

Easter Crosses

CRAFTY TIPS ✔ Instead of using candy sprinkles, try placing the "sticky" crosses in bags of paper confetti, colored popcorn, or rice.

SIMPLE SUPPLIES

You'll need craft sticks, tacky craft glue, scissors, pie pans, candy sprinkles, cotton swabs, a hot-glue gun, self-adhesive magnetic strip, and a blow-dryer.

DIRECTIONS

❶ Before class use a hot-glue gun to glue two wooden craft sticks together in the shape of a cross. Cut self-adhesive magnetic strip into 1-inch lengths. Prepare a wooden cross and magnetic strip for each child.

❷ Set out cotton swabs and pie pans of candy sprinkles and tacky craft glue. Hand each child a wooden cross and a cotton swab. Have each child spread a thick layer of glue on one side of the craft stick cross.

❸ Show children how to carefully place their crosses, glue-side down, in the pan of candy sprinkles. Then help children take turns holding a blow-dryer to dry their decorated projects. Be sure the blow-dryer is set on low.

❹ When the crosses are dry, stick pieces of magnetic strip on the backs to make refrigerator magnets.

EXTRA FUN

Remind children that Jesus died on the cross so we could be God's friends. Tell children that their special magnets will help them remember how much Jesus loves us. And just like a magnet, Jesus pulls us close to him with love.

Challenge children to explore placing their magnets on objects around the room. Then teach children the following rhyme.

Jesus is with me, you know. *(Point up.)*
He holds me tight *(clasp your hands together)*
And won't let go! *(Pretend to try to pull your hands apart.)*

Confetti Eggs

SIMPLE SUPPLIES

You'll need colored construction paper, white construction paper, a hole punch, scissors, plastic bowls, tacky craft glue, cotton swabs, and pastel yarn.

DIRECTIONS

❶ Before class cut pastel yarn into 6-inch lengths. Cut one length of yarn for each child. You may also wish to get a head start on punching out colored confetti bits with a hole punch and construction paper.

❷ Set out white construction paper, tacky craft glue, yarn, cotton swabs, plastic bowls, colored construction paper, and a hole punch. Let children take turns punching out confetti from the colored paper. Place the confetti in plastic bowls.

❸ Give each child a sheet of white construction paper, then show children how to tear out large oval egg shapes.

❹ Demonstrate how to use a cotton swab to brush glue on one side of a paper egg, then invite children to spread glue on their own eggs.

❺ When the glue is spread around the paper egg shapes, have children take confetti and sprinkle it over their eggs, then shake off the excess confetti.

❻ Punch a hole in the top of each decorated egg and tie a piece of yarn through the hole for a hanger. Allow the paper eggs to dry for five minutes.

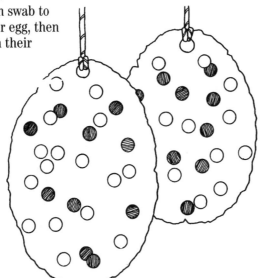

CRAFTY TIPS

✔ Spray the confetti-covered eggs with hair spray to add a bit of shine and to help confetti stay securely attached.

✔ Try using snippets of colored craft feathers to coat the eggs for a tactile twist.

EXTRA FUN

After the paper eggs are dry, lead children in this fun action rhyme. Form groups of five and have children sit down holding their eggs in front of them. As you act out the rhyme together, have children sit down one by one until only one "egg" is left in each group.

Five little eggs were sitting on the floor. *(Show five fingers.)*
One fell out *(roll on your side),*
And then there were four. *(Hold up four fingers.)*

Four little eggs were sitting in a tree. *(Show four fingers.)*
One fell out *(roll on your side),*
And then there were three. *(Hold up three fingers.)*

Three little were eggs feeling blue.
One fell out *(roll on your side),*
And then there were two. *(Hold up two fingers.)*

Two little were eggs looking for fun.
One fell out *(roll on your side),*
And then there was one. *(Hold up one finger.)*

One little egg, we're almost done.
When it falls out *(roll on your side),*
There will be none. *(Shake your head)*

Red, White, and Blue Cookies

CRAFTY TIPS

✔ Older preschoolers may want to pat a larger piece of dough into a rectangle and drop in candies to form a flag pattern.

✔ Have each child make two or three cookies. Let children decorate a table with red and blue streamers and invite their parents to share the treats.

SIMPLE SUPPLIES

You'll need wax paper, a hammer or meat mallet, aluminum foil, a plastic knife, small margarine tubs, refrigerated sugar-cookie dough, a cookie sheet, and red and blue hard candies. You'll also need access to an oven.

DIRECTIONS

❶ Before class use a hammer or meat mallet to crush the hard candies.

❷ Set the candy pieces in small margarine tubs.

❸ Line the cookie sheet with aluminum foil.

❹ Slice refrigerated cookie dough onto a sheet of wax paper. You'll need one slice for each child.

❺ Let children take turns placing a circle of dough on the cookie sheet then pressing small pieces of hard candies into the dough.

❻ Bake the cookies according to package directions. The hard candies will melt into glittering spots of color.
Caution the children not to touch because the hard candies will remain hot for a few minutes.

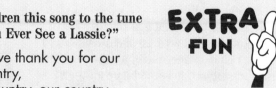

Teach children this song to the tune of "Did You Ever See a Lassie?"

Lord, we thank you for our country,
Our country, our country.
Lord, we thank you for our country,
A land strong and free.

God bless you, God bless me,
And God bless our country.
Lord, we thank you for our country,
A land strong and free.

Sing and march around the classroom as the cookies bake. After their marching and singing, children will be ready for a cool glass of lemonade with their warm, sparkly cookies!

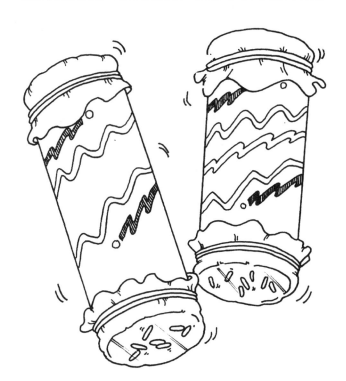

A Noisy Nation

SIMPLE SUPPLIES

You'll need cardboard bathroom-tissue tubes, scissors, red and blue markers, construction paper, glue sticks, clear packing tape, wax paper, rubber bands, uncooked rice, and plastic spoons.

DIRECTIONS

❶ Before class collect cardboard bathroom-tissue tubes or make a 6-inch cardboard tube for each child. Cut wax paper into 4-inch squares. You'll need two squares for each child.

❷ Give each child a cardboard tube and set the other supplies on a table.

❸ Show children how to place a square of wax paper on one end of a tube, then use a rubber band to secure it. Double-check to make sure the children's rubber bands are on securely, then wrap clear packing tape over the rubber bands.

❹ Have each child pour two spoonfuls of rice into his or her tube. Then help children fasten squares of wax paper on the open end of their tubes. Secure the wax paper with rubber bands and clear packing tape.

❺ Invite children to decorate their noisemakers with bits of construction paper and colorful markers.

CRAFTY TIPS

✔ Dry beans or small pebbles can be substituted for rice, but be sure both ends of the noisemaker tube are closed securely with rubber bands and tape.

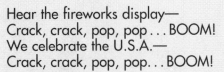

Let children joyously shake, rattle, and roll their noisemakers as you lead them in this snappy song to the tune of "Old MacDonald Had a Farm."

Hear the fireworks display—
Crack, crack, pop, pop… BOOM!
We celebrate the U.S.A.—
Crack, crack, pop, pop… BOOM!

With a bing, bang here
And a crash, boom there—
Sparkling in the air,
Fireworks are everywhere!

Hear the fireworks display—
Crack, crack, pop, pop… BOOM!

Hidden Turkeys

CRAFTY TIPS

✔ Make a Christmas adaptation of the traditional stacking folk dolls by decorating the paper cups as angels.

✔ Use this craft idea while learning about Noah's ark. Use the large paper cup for an ark and the two smaller cups for animals sailing inside the ark.

SIMPLE SUPPLIES

You'll need party-favor nut cups, 8-ounce paper cups, 12-ounce paper cups, craft feathers or construction paper, markers, and tape.

DIRECTIONS

❶ Set out tape, craft feathers or construction paper, and markers. Give each child a nut cup. Encourage children to tape craft feathers or construction paper "tail feathers" on the cups to make turkeys.

❷ Show children how to use markers to make eyes and beaks.

❸ Give each child an 8-ounce cup and a 12-ounce cup. Instruct children to make larger turkeys in the same way they made the smaller ones.

❹ When each child has finished making three turkeys, stack the gobblers one on top of the other. Let children stack and restack their turkey friends.

EXTRA FUN

Have children stack their turkeys and use them to help tell this silly story. For added fun, have children "gobble" each time they hear the word "turkey."

I found a little turkey
Hiding out, as turkeys do.
But when I picked the turkey up *(lift first cup)*,
Surprise! There were two.
I was about to take my new friends
Home to play with me.
But when I picked them both up *(raise both turkeys)*,
Surprise! There were three.
I was just so blessed,
As blessed as blessed can be.
Not one turkey for Thanksgiving,
But one, two, three. *(Stack the turkeys back up.)*

Precious Pumpkins

SIMPLE SUPPLIES

You'll need brown paper lunch bags, scissors, newspaper, green string or yarn, green chenille wire, orange and green tempera paint, pie pans, paint shirts, and paintbrushes.

DIRECTIONS

❶ Before class cover your work area with newspaper. Have children wear paint shirts or paper grocery sacks with holes cut out for arms and heads.
Cut green yarn into 8-inch lengths, providing one for each child. Also cut chenille wire into 10-inch lengths. You'll need one for each child.

❷ Set out newspaper. Distribute the paper bags and have children stuff the bags with crumpled newspaper to make pudgy pumpkins.

❸ Tell children to leave enough room at the top to close the bags. Tie the tops of bags with green yarn to create pumpkin stalks.

❹ Set out paintbrushes and pie pans containing green and orange tempera paint. Let children paint the pumpkins orange and the stalks green.

❺ Carefully wrap green chenille wires around the stalks and curl the ends to make pumpkin vines. Allow the pumpkins to dry for 20 minutes.

CRAFTY TIPS

✔ This rhyme can also be used as a finger play. Make pumpkin faces on fingertips and thumbs. Have each child hold up all 10 fingers. Begin the rhyme with "Ten pudgy pumpkins..." Then each time you repeat the rhyme, tuck one finger into your palm until no fingers are showing.

✔ When the pumpkins are completely dry, you may wish to let children tear out and glue on black construction paper eyes, noses, and smiling mouths.

EXTRA FUN

When the pumpkins are dry, set them on the floor in a row. Lead children in the following rhyme. As you repeat the last line, choose a child to remove his or her pumpkin from the "pumpkin patch," and hold it while the rhyme is repeated. Continue until no pumpkins are left in the pumpkin patch.

If the pumpkins are still wet or if you'd like to put a twist on the rhyme, have children pretend to be the pumpkins in the patch. On the last line, tap a child on the shoulder to step out of the pumpkin patch and hold hands with you. Repeat until all the children have been "picked."

(Number) pudgy pumpkins all in a row.
God loved them all and helped them grow.
The day finally came to pick one, you see?
And away went the pumpkin quick as can be!

Turkey Gobblers

CRAFTY TIPS

✔ You may want to give children a little extra dough to munch on as they create their turkeys.

✔ If children choose to eat their turkeys right away, encourage them not to eat more than half—the dough is quite rich and you don't want any turkey tummy-aches!

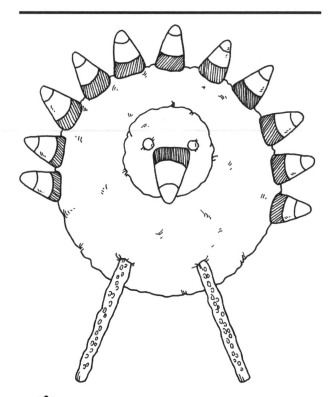

SIMPLE SUPPLIES

You'll need peanut butter, plastic bowls, powdered sugar, a mixing bowl, a spoon, a measuring cup, small paper plates, pretzel sticks, candy corn, and wet wipes.

DIRECTIONS

❶ Before class mix a 1-pound box of powdered sugar with a 16-ounce jar of peanut butter. Add powdered sugar until the dough is no longer sticky.
❷ Set out bowls of candy corn and pretzels.
❸ Make sure children wash their hands before they begin this craft.
❹ Give each child a small paper plate and about ⅛ cup of dough.
❺ Have each child pinch off a quarter-sized piece of the dough and set it aside for the head.
❻ Demonstrate how to pat the dough into an oval mound for the turkey's body and add pretzel-stick legs.
❼ Let children press candy corn around the top of the bodies for feathers.
❽ Finally have each child make a circle with the dough he or she set aside for a head, press the head in place on top of the body, and add another piece of candy corn for a beak.
❾ Have children use wet wipes to clean their hands as soon as they've finished their turkey creations.
Children may eat their treats or save them as table decorations. The dough doesn't need to be refrigerated—it will remain fresh and edible for several days.

EXTRA FUN

Talk about how American Indian friends helped the pilgrims gather food for their first Thanksgiving dinner. Explain that God wants people to help each other and to give thanks.

Teach children this simple Thanksgiving game. Have children sit in a circle on the floor. To begin the game, you'll be the gobbler. Walk around the outside of the circle and say "gobble" as you touch each person's shoulder. When you touch a child and say "Thanks," that child stands up and finishes the sentence, "I thank God for…" Then that child becomes the gobbler and you sit in his or her place. Continue until each child has had a turn being the gobbler.

"I thank my God every time I remember you, always praying with joy for all of you" (Philippians 1:3-4).

Prayer Pals

SIMPLE SUPPLIES

You'll need rocks, tempera paint, pie pans, paintbrushes, newspaper, paint shirts, felt scraps, paper scraps, markers, dot stickers, paper towels, and tacky craft glue.

DIRECTIONS

❶ Begin this activity by taking your class out to collect rocks. Encourage children to choose flat rocks about the size of an apple.

❷ Cover your work area with newspaper. Have children wear paint shirts or paper grocery sacks with holes cut out for arms and heads.

❸ Set out tempera paint in pie pans, paintbrushes, glue, and other items. Encourage children to decorate their rocks with felt scraps, paper, and paint.

❹ When children have completed decorating, give them dot stickers to add as eyes. Show them how to use a marker to put little dots inside the stickers to make googly eyes for their Prayer Pals.

❺ Allow rocks to dry for 15 minutes before handling. If tempera paint is thick, allow additional drying time or blot off excess with a paper towel.

CRAFTY TIPS

✔ Prayer Pals may be made as gifts any time during the year. Kept on a desk or counter top, they're a great prayer reminder.

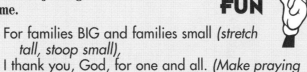

Have children hold their Prayer Pals while joining in this thankful rhyme.

EXTRA FUN

For families BIG and families small *(stretch tall, stoop small),*
I thank you, God, for one and all. *(Make praying hands.)*

Repeat the rhyme, allowing children to take turns telling something they're thankful for such as parents, a new bike, or friends.